Seeking Inner Peace

Dr. Alfred Nkut

AuthorHouse™
1663 Liberty Drive
Bloomington, IN 47403
www.authorhouse.com
Phone: 1-800-839-8640

First published by AuthorHouse 6/4/2010

ISBN: 978-1-4520-3321-1 (sc)

Printed in the United States of America
Bloomington, Indiana

This book is printed on acid-free paper.

authorHOUSE®

To

Lise

[signature]

This book is dedicated to my wife, Elaine Blacklock,
and to our children, Ruthie and Jacob, for their goodness of heart.

Acknowledgments

I extend my deepest thanks to:

Jessica Lachance, my assistant. You are more than an assistant.
Thank you for your editorial insight and shared vision.

My brilliant and insightful editors at AuthorHouse.

Daniela Flores, my graphic designer, for the book cover
and illustrations. Your work is impeccable.

Introduction

Joy may come from within, but knowing this does not seem to fuel people to try to find it. Why? I wish the answer were simple and could fit into a small box tied with a ribbon; but people are different and seek diverse spiritual paths for personal fulfillment. Because of this, what brings joy to one person may not resonate with another.

Learning how you can raise your level of inner satisfaction is the essence of this book. This book refers to a person's joy or inner satisfaction as inner peace. It is happiness of the spirit that results from an absence of anxiety within. I think this is true happiness, because it comes from the internal and natural source—the soul. Unlike pleasure, inner peace does not depend on an external source; it is happiness of the body.

My experience and research working with people coping with life challenges are the basis for this book. In my clinic, I have interviewed hundreds of people on how they dealt with difficulties in their lives. After so many interviews, I have the conviction that one does not have to be battered in a storm before learning what to do when faced with one. We build inner strength knowing that challenges come unannounced.

An important aspect to maintaining inner satisfaction is to accept what life sets in front of you, even if you do not like it, because resisting any situation is a surefire recipe for attracting psychological suffering onto oneself. Being motivated and ambitious, and pursuing one's interests, can be very exciting, especially if you do it for the joy of it and are not motivated by the rat race or a competitive struggle. In order to acquire such a mindset, we have to see every day as a blessing.

I think that seeking inner peace is an essential part of spiritual growth—yet, like all things, we have to be motivated and want to do it.

Master the principles that I will share in this book on how to tap into an inner source of boundless joy, and life will become automatically better.

People can find the keys for becoming master artists in cultivating inner peace. Our power lies in programming our mind for joy. And this can be achieved by following the path that is laid out in this book.

1. How to Generate Positive Emotions

Chapter 1:

How to Generate Positive Emotions

"Everything begins with a thought."

- Ralph Waldo Emerson

I first saw Jake at an initial visit for my study and came to know him through many follow-up visits during which interviews were conducted. Jake had worked at the same job for many years. He said that he enjoyed it until his new boss was hired.

His new boss was appointed to a job that was not in the boss's area of expertise; as such, the responsibility of teaching him the job fell to Jake. Jake had to explain everything to him numerous times and even use pictures to explain certain tasks before the boss could comprehend them. Jake said that he felt like he was talking to a ten-year-old. "A real dummy," he said.

There was hardly any positive experience in Jake's life, and he rationalized it by blaming the boss for his frustration. He didn't have anything positive to say about his family—either his spouse or his children. Everything was about him, which was a very self-centered view of life. He thought that if everybody could just change, his life would become better. He told me that his love for life and interests would return if those conditions were met.

After many visits with Jake, I realized that I was not getting anywhere; we had not made much progress toward making him happier. Therefore, I suggested therapy sessions with a great psychologist who focused on helping people who wanted to be happier. Unfortunately, the many sessions of therapy did not seem to change Jake's level of happiness. He was still very bored and gloomy about life. His get-up-and-go attitude was still lost.

One day, Jake came to see me because he was feeling low. He had a new story to tell me about how miserable he was feeling. He had a long list of new problems, and he still felt that the reason for his unhappiness was the world around him: "If people would just become a little bit reasonable, life would be better." If his grandchildren would just behave, he would feel much better. His attitude had not changed.

It was during another interview with Jake that he opened my mind about how he was feeling . At the end of the session, I noticed that he had not mentioned the issues with his new boss once during the whole interaction. This was very unusual because it had been his standard issue for some time. Because of this, I posed the question, "How is your boss doing?"

He hesitated. It seemed he was trying to conceal that his boss had passed away, which, for me, begged the question, why was he not feeling better?

"He passed away," Jake said with pause. "I mean this man was a very good man." He did not say it in such a way as to suggest that it was good that the boss had passed away. He said it with a sigh of regret.

I asked about the cause of the boss's unfortunate passing. It was a sudden death of unknown cause. And, many months after he had died, Jake's unhappiness did not improve.

I interviewed many people with stories similar to Jake's, but his grabbed my attention. Why, despite the passing of Jake's boss, did his level of happiness not improve? It speaks to how irrational emotions can be.

This observation is further compounded by the people that I interviewed who had very similar negative life circumstances but were living a life of personal fulfillment and satisfaction while others were not. *What could be the reason for the difference,* I wondered.

The common denominator in a good number of those situations was that they all had a victim mentality—they all thought that they were defenseless in one way or another. The explanation for their feelings of unhappiness was not from within, but from outside influences—the world!

Jake hardly sees himself as a winner. No. He sees himself as losing, whether it is about the present or the past. He sees limitations, not the possibilities that victors see. He minimizes all the good that has happened in his life and magnifies all the negative experiences.

Despite the fact that Jake has kept a very good job for many years, he still sees himself as merely getting by financially.

Two main reasons seemed to explain the apparent contradiction observed over time in Jake. First, he did not have the ability to cope with life challenges. Second, he wrongly identified with his apparent setback, which was the falling out with his boss; he let it consume his entire life. He did not have the stomach to digest adversity, which is an important quality needed for staying happy, because, sooner or later, we all come across something that we do not like in life.

He did not have the ability to generate positive emotions either. This is paramount in making oneself happy, and it is explained in detail throughout this book. Many elements are involved with maintaining inner peace in our lives. Self-image is the key, because self-image is the anchor of emotions. Our image flows from our thoughts, and the thoughts that we harbor emanate from our identity.

Self-Image

In order to understand how to generate positive emotions, you must understand how they are related to image. We all have a picture of ourselves in our minds. This self-image is either positive or negative, depending on our internal dialogue. A negative internal dialogue generates a negative self-image, whereas a positive internal dialogue gives a positive self-image.

Why is self-image so important? Motivational speaker and author Bob Proctor provides the best explanation. He describes thoughts such as self-image to be like a thermostat in a room. The thermostat is set at a certain temperature that it cannot surpass. In the same way, your thoughts or your self-image sets the standard at which you will function. You cannot rise higher than the image that you have of yourself. So if we think back to Jake, he was unhappy because he had a negative self-image. How could he have changed the dynamics? By creating a positive self-image.

The Emotional Flow Chart

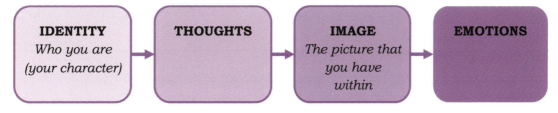

People feel unhappy because they think negative thoughts. That creates a negative self-image. Jake was unhappy because he had a negative self-image. His internal dialogue was negative. In order to change his self-image, Jake first had to change his internal dialogue simply by choosing positive thoughts, because feelings come from the image that we all have within. Thoughts create the images that we have of ourselves.

It is important to be in alignment with your identity if you want to live in harmony with who you really are.

Your identity is who you are, your character, including the qualities that form your core beliefs, such as integrity and discipline.

A chapter in this book is dedicated to how the mind works and techniques like visualization that are used for creating positive emotions. In order to change your internal dialogue from a negative to a positive one, you have to make a conscious effort to choose positive thoughts. It does not come spontaneously. It is not automatic. It needs cultivation.

You can speak positive words of victory to yourself all the time. You can make affirmations that support what you want to change in your life. The mind works by affirmation, which means that it can only say yes. And so, as it does not know how to say no. Affirmations have to be positive. For example, to make a change from a victim to a victor mentality, you can say, "I am a victor." Tell yourself that long enough, and through the repetition your subconscious mind will help supplant it for you. This process is called conditioning, and it is this unending learning and unlearning that builds our inner strength.

Minding our belief system is important, because the mind is like a vacuum, which means you can feed it with almost anything.

Living in harmony with who you are is important. When you are not in harmony, you can let your life happen by chance or default.

Another important technique discussed in subsequent chapters in this book is visualization. It is simply seeing yourself be whatever it is that you expect or want. Jake did not see himself as happy. His picture within was a dark one.

Develop a Happiness Consciousness

We are always making choices, even if we do so in an unconscious manner. Be an active participant in shaping how you feel. An inner voice of wisdom can do a lot of prompting through hunches. We can make good choices if we listen to our gut feelings.

Imagine how the room temperature would fluctuate if there were no thermostat. This example underscores the importance of our continual awareness of what we desire. We have to cultivate this awareness. It is not automatic.

Inner peace is a great fruit that needs hard work to harvest. On a day-to-day basis, we can actively think about things that can be done to enhance it. Do whatever it takes. I find morning devotions with a good book and pen and paper very effective for building my inner strength. Read whatever appeals to you. I particularly enjoy biographical books and scripture.

Why the pen and paper? Later in this book, I discuss the brainstorming technique; it stimulates creativity, and the flow of ideas from the brain becomes almost spontaneous as soon as I start writing. For some people, journaling works very well. Brainstorming is definitely part of it, because writing is involved, but it has also been said that anything that gets thoughts and feelings out in the open, either positive or negative, is good for you. Try to get the poison (negative thoughts and feelings) out of your mind. The positive thoughts, when put on paper, can be appreciated even more.

From a psycho-spiritual perspective, if the mind were to function without guiding and redirecting our attention, we would become irrational. In order to make use of our thinking, it has to be focused—directed at a particular goal or intention. This process will be explained in detail in subsequent chapters.

Understanding Loneliness

Far too many people have asked me why they feel lonely. It is not easy to explain, because it is a feeling. Feelings can be irrational, and thus very difficult to explain.

Just as we can only dodge a pothole when we are aware of its existence, it is important to know what loneliness is so that we can avoid it. From a spiritual perspective, this awareness is like light. Why? Because awareness has the potential to make ignorance disappear, in the same way that light makes darkness disappear.

So conscious awareness is very powerful. I would say that it is more powerful than ignorance. Ignorance tends to fuel fear and doubt, which are precursors of negative feelings.

Loneliness is an emotional separation that comes from social withdrawal. One thing I found with Jake was that he was emotionally introverted—which means that his feelings were turned inward, rather than outward into the world.

Jake confided in me that he used to be joyous and outgoing until his infamous boss came into the picture. After failed attempts to get along with him, Jake gave up. Like many people who are extremely unhappy, Jake withdrew from the uncomfortable situation with his boss. He withdrew into his comfort zone. Quite often, this is a false sense of security that is motivated by selfishness, superiority, or an inferiority complex. A simple example is someone who feels he or she is better than everyone else because of material riches, or someone who has had a major loss or misfortune and feels ashamed to meet with people and goes into hiding at home. The problem with withdrawal from people is that it leads to emotional separation—and ultimately loneliness.

Jake was happy until he had to work with a boss that he did not like. He started slipping backward as he lost his confidence. Despair set in as feelings of inadequacy predominated his life. He started feeling a knot and butterflies in his stomach, symptoms of anxiety that can accompany extreme unhappiness, stress, or depression.

A great secret for staying happy is to simply defy the odds by simply refusing to think and feel negative thoughts, constantly redirecting your attention to the victorious mindset. This is very powerful; it will help you to stay afloat.

Even when negative experiences happen, people must accept the fact that life is a continual challenge, and obstacles are part of the puzzle. Refusing to dwell on negative experiences is the key to maintaining inner peace.

An uplifted spirit gives us inner strength, which is a buffer for any storms that may come our way. It also makes the neurotransmitters in our bodies shoot out happy chemicals like serotonin, which makes you happier.

Defying negative thoughts or feelings is simply saying, "No, I am not going down into that hole." But a person has to first acknowledge them before letting them go. That release is a necessity, so do not repress negative feelings by denying them.

There is nothing wrong with feeling angry about a situation that is frustrating or grieving about a major loss. These are normal emotions that when harnessed the right way can actually give people psychological and emotional relief. Take time to grieve a loss. See an expert, such as a grief counselor, to help you if it is necessary.

Eventually you must let go of the loss and refocus on the positive aspects of life, otherwise the loss becomes "baggage." It weighs heavily and crowds one's mind, to the point that some depressed people say they feel as if their heads will explode. This is because their feelings are directed inward; they are living in their head rather than out in the world.

Be emotionally prepared. No matter what happens, beat the odds and move forward. By doing that, a person gains the habit of staying on the bright side of life, not the dark side. In the survey I conducted, that was a key characteristic that set happy and unhappy people apart.

When we find ourselves feeling empty or in a hole, we don't want to stay there forever. We can simply snap out of it. Using conscious awareness helps us to move onto something better. Changing our internal dialogue from negative to positive will tip our energy balance positively. It is the primary thing to do to get ourselves out of the hole. Even if we supplant something positive in our minds as simple as feeling good about our next meal, it will make a difference as we begin to move forward. But people are very creative; we can do better than that. The best way to get rid of a negative thought is to substitute another thought—a positive thought—for it. You cannot dismiss a thought directly. But you can replace it, simply by substituting a positive thought for it. This works because the conscious mind can hold only one thought at a time.

How to Create Excitement

Thoughts can be set like a thermostat to invite anything, spiritual or material, into one's life. A person can invite panic or calm into his or her life with thoughts.

Jake was the creator of the prison cell for himself, not his boss. He was inviting a lot of misery onto himself. The use of his conscious awareness to make choices for himself was his primary leverage. Instead, he wanted the boss to change. It was an impossible task.

A person can constantly use imagination to fill his or her heart with uplifting thoughts and feelings. Babies are always conceived before they are born. Do the same thing. Create the picture of what is desired within—an image. See yourself in the role that you are seeking. Make affirmations on the wonderful things that you want to do. Those are the things that yield personal fulfillment, not only when they are achieved, but on the journey to achieving them, which can be just as interesting.

Make affirmation on good feelings: "I feel good about myself" or "I am very excited about my project on ..." Repeat these positive statements all day long and just before falling asleep.

Visualize happiness—smiling, walking with a spring in your step, holding hands with your dream partner. And it does not stop there. No. Go out and do the wonderful things that you are dreaming of. We become generous not only by thinking generous, but by acting generous. Start smiling now! In the beginning, it is a little tough to initiate, but make a habit of smiling and laughing all the time. That bit of acting rubs off on you very quickly, and, sooner or later, it becomes a habit.

Uplifting thoughts greatly influence a person's body chemistry. Neurotransmitters secrete more happy chemicals like serotonin. Modest quantities of adrenaline start thumping though the body. In short, they positively tip your energy balance, and you feel energetic.

Two people observe water in a glass. One of them says the glass is half full, the other says it is half empty. The two people are right. The difference is that the first observer is creating a positive image, and the second observer is creating a negative image. One is striving to stay on the bright side, and that is more powerful than staying in the dark side where the glass is half empty.

Thoughts and words are energy. Positive thoughts and words carry positive energy. And negative thoughts and words carry negative energy. Negative thoughts and words will suck your energy.

Knowing that, a person should fill his or her mind with thoughts and words that carry positive energy. These positive thoughts will make that person feel more buoyant. Why not expect the best, rather than the worst? Well, expectations can be surpassed, and nothing will be lost expecting the best. Always think that the best is yet to come.

Jake could have counted his good health, his job, his spouse, and his children as a blessing. What would he have lost if doing that made him feel better?

Thoughts and feelings can be set on unconditional acceptance rather than hate, on confidence rather than fear. When the mind is preoccupied with compassion that is what will manifest in the external world. Plant seeds of confidence by thinking, acting, and feeling confident. These could be just simple gestures of compassion, helping, or giving in any form—spiritually or materially. I see nice words to someone as spiritual giving.

Fear will refuel doubt and timidity. And that is the picture that will be created within. People who fear will feel shy and then retreat from action or withdraw into their comfort zone where they feel safe.

If you are feeling either low or bored, chances are that you are giving your attention to something negative, whether it is real or imagined.

The key to changing these dynamics is to start seeing the world beyond your needs. That will open new doors and generate creativity and new ideas.

As soon as you start filling your mind with exciting new ideas, they will crowd out the old mental clutter. You will start feeling like a new person.

There are always things to be excited about, from thoughts about a next meal to the wonderful things we dream about doing with our lives. And getting out and doing those things that we are interested in will further generate more excitement in our lives.

2. How to Become Mentally Tough

Chapter 2:

How to Become Mentally Tough

"I find deep inner peace within myself as I am."

- Anonymous

Amanda is a lady who sought counsel because she was not coping well anywhere in her life. When I first met her, she expressed regret for not doing what could be described as a "calling." She was still in search of Mr. Right too, as she had just broken up with Mr. Wrong. These were her words: "It all began with a terrible childhood." She recounted memories of parents who wanted her to live the great dreams that they should have pursued but did not. She was pressured into making career choices that were inappropriate, simply in an attempt to pacify them and keep the peace at home. Both of her parents were in a constant battle as to whose choice of a career she was going to adopt.

She confided to me that her life was ravaged by panic attacks. Her anxiety was obvious—she looked uneasy, avoided eye contact, and had sweaty palms.

Conversations during interviews are very revealing. They reveal the microcosm of how people conduct their lives. For example, observing Amanda panicking, simply tells the story that she feels overwhelmed internally. Also, when she heard something that she did not like, she got very defensive and hysterical rather than taking it in stride. She couldn't move onto positive energy conversations or ideas that were stimulating, and that drew people in, rather than alienating them.

I noticed a general pattern with Amanda. Rather than facing the issues in her life by taking responsibility, she tried to blame the world for everything that happened to her since childhood.

I could just see Amanda holding a deck of victim cards in her hands. She played them all along. That was her only game. She was skillful in playing the victim mentality as she spent time divulging lots of her baggage in a false attempt to get sympathy. The focus of our interaction was supposed to be for Amanda, together with me, to explore and understand why she was having problems in her life. That is, a way to understand who she is.

These sessions were supposed to provide guidance for her to learn how to allow her own inner wisdom to flow until she could intuitively listen to her inner voice, otherwise she could not release her innate potential.

What Defines You?

We all possess an identity. It is who we are, formed of the character traits that we have, like confidence, persistence, and resilience. Image is the picture that we carry in our mind. Our behavior, actions, and emotions flow from this image within.

In order to live in harmony, your behavior should flow from your image, and your image from your identity.

Being in alignment with those three areas gives you a firm, authentic, and predictable way of thinking and acting. You can build your character using a belief system and values of your choice. Mental conditioning, by continually challenging the mind with these beliefs over time, creates and strengthens your self-image, which represents your reality.

Your ability to succeed in any area of your life, including inner peace, is framed in character traits. Resilience gives you mental toughness because it is your ability to recover quickly from a setback. This is crucial, as most people do very well until something happens that they do not like. When they react to it rather than acting responsibly, despair sets in and they lose their confidence. And if they do not quickly return to their former state using resilience, they can remain stuck in a valley of unhappiness.

Persistence is needed to keep making an effort despite difficulties. I have gone through thick and thin in life, and I know beyond a doubt that life is a series of continual challenges. Expecting them, and in some way seeing them as opportunities and blessings rather than a curse, creates a very positive mental attitude. Nothing is actually lost until you feel it is lost. This quality helps you to keep going, no matter what!

Of course, confidence is the belief in your abilities. "Everything we do begins with a thought," said Ralph Waldo Emerson. Come to think about it, having faith in ourselves, and even better into something beyond ourselves, is very important too. Lack of confidence makes us fearful and timid about moving forward. So we become bored, we lack adventure. We procrastinate all day long in attempting an action, partly because we feel inadequate about the possibility of succeeding.

The Character Flow Chart

In essence, the image we have of ourselves is what defines us. The picture has to be very clear in our minds. We will always be confused about what we want to become, or enjoy, until a firm identity has been visualized and planted within.

Oprah Winfrey says that what defines us is how we treat ourselves and others. Whatever resonates with your personal philosophy should be your identity.

Our identity is not static because we constantly learn new things, grow, and mature. So conditioning is an unending process. We should constantly think that we could do better, as we become more curious and imaginative. It is very healthy because it makes us interested and interesting. Such stimulation makes life more exciting—and this brings happiness. Boredom will accrue when there is nothing that sustains our interest, and that is tantamount to unhappiness. The feeling of inner control leads to feeling good.

I do not feel bad when I find someone at any age who is confused about life like Amanda. I used to, but I find that growth and maturity is a continuous process. And too, I do not think that I am even halfway through my own evolution. Why? Because it was at age forty-two, in 2007, that I decided to be a motivational writer. It came because of my fascination with leadership and feelings. I had often toyed about writing, but I did not know exactly what I was going to write about until 2007.

The Character Flow Chart

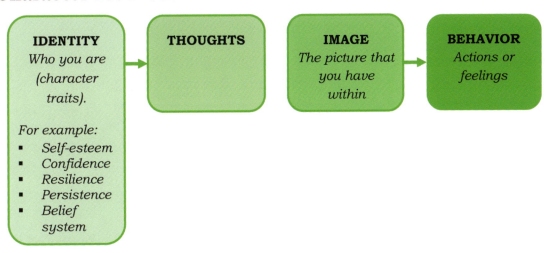

IDENTITY
Who you are
(character
traits).

For example:
- Self-esteem
- Confidence
- Resilience
- Persistence
- Belief
  system

THOUGHTS

IMAGE
The picture that
you have
within

BEHAVIOR
Actions or
feelings

Most of the qualities that we use to cope with challenges are character traits. They are foundational to our existence because our self-image flows from them, and our feelings as well. Self-image is important because we think, act, and feel as we conceive ourselves to be. The way we feel inside determines how we look on the outside unless we are putting on a mask. To put on a bold face, image you are bold inside. It is easier to walk with a spring in your step if that is the picture you have within.

Mirror exercises to build inner strength are going to be discussed later—as well as using a blueprint of character traits you desire to develop a magnetic character.

Here is why character is important. You can best understand this by comparing commitment and discipline. Commitment is the pledge for a course of action, while discipline is the practice of imposing strict rules of behavior. It is easy to make lofty promises; the problem is to follow through. People can say who they want to be, but are they really who they say they are? The gap between the two is what constitutes reality, and reality is the difference between what you wish and what is.

Amanda was asked to do self-evaluation on how disciplined she was. On a scale of one to ten, she had a three. At first, she felt victimized. She was feeling overwhelmed. She felt inadequate as well. This drew psychological suffering to her. Why? Because the anxiety she was going through was obvious.

Through repeated practice to increase her confidence level and strengthen her ability to cope with adversity, her confidence level increased. So did her inner strength. She became much less nervous. She could actually go out and try new things, like dating, which she initially dreaded. By her own admission, once she could not stand the thought of someone saying no to her. Now she can.

With time, Amanda improved her discipline from a three to a seven on a scale of one to ten. She was exuding more confidence later on because she felt stronger inside. She became a magnet of happiness, as she could now attract even more of it. She reported that her whining and complaining actually reduced, because her negative self-image changed to a positive one. Her world within changed, so the world outside also changed.

Inner peace needs cultivation. It does not come automatically. So, get disciplined, and practice what defines you until it becomes a habit.

Believe in Your Abilities

The way we interpret events is primarily a projection of the image from within—self-image. Self-image is the anchor of our emotions, which flows from our identity.

After many counseling sessions with Amanda, it became obvious that she did not believe in her innate abilities. Having faith in oneself is very important because our thoughts dwell on what we believe in, and over time they create the picture within, which becomes our reality.

Thoughts of unworthiness and inadequacy come from not believing in one's abilities. This creates a negative self-image, which generates feelings of inadequacy. If you feel that you are not able, then it leads to being overwhelmed, which could make you easily frightened. That is how timidity is born. Toxic emotions of fear, doubt, and guilt also result from that negative self-image.

Thoughts of inadequacy draw suffering onto you through these toxic emotions. Unhappiness ensues when the soul (your joy) is encumbered by those toxic emotions.

The key is to change your internal dialogue from negative to positive, supplanting a negative self-image with positive one, from which your feelings will flow.

So fill your heart with positive images—things that you can do, things that you like. Use your imagination to help you. In order to do this you have to will happiness, and then create it. "All things begin with a thought," as Ralph Waldo Emerson noted. Simply visualize yourself happy. See yourself sitting at your favorite holiday destination.

In order to release your innate potential, including inner peace, you have to use your creativity. It begins with curiosity to learn new ideas. Learning stimulates the brain, and people often learn things that they are interested in, which leads to more excitement. And, learning improves your awareness and tends to drive out the ignorance that inspires doubt and fear, which are very toxic emotions.

How to Deal with Setbacks

One of Amanda's Achilles' heels was that she was often overwhelmed with everything. The wrinkles on her face were obvious. Even when she did smile, her mouth did not touch her ears. All along as we went through counseling sessions, I noticed that she lacked confidence. The very idea of coming out of her safe place to date with another person made her sweat, she confided. It took her psychologist an uncountable number of sessions to get her ready for the experience of dating once more after she broke up with her partner. The psychologist asked her that if she had a child, and it died, wouldn't she give birth to another child? The obvious answer was yes. It was not a deterrent for not having another child. She told me that she learned that the hard way. Amanda did not have the stomach to digest setbacks, so instead, she identified with them, and they took over her whole life. They became her self-image.

She spent a lot of time divulging her baggage in a false attempt to get sympathy. One's internal dialogue and self-image are one's universe because that is where the external world is created from. Amanda was not feeling good about herself, so even getting married to a saint would not change her! What needed changing was her internal dialogue and self-image.

People who feel confident carry on positive energy conversations that tend to draw in others. It is unlike those who lack confidence, like Amanda, with the victim mentality. What was happening within was that she felt inadequate and that is what she projected to her outer world.

When Amanda learned through the mirror exercises to improve her self-image, she started orchestrating positive energy conversations while dating, and that changed her whole dating experience.

People with a victim mentality tend to try to tear down others, because misery loves company. And you cannot give out more than you have. Never blame such a person, instead feel sorry for them. They are filled with toxic emotions of doubt, fear, and guilt, and the poison is all they have to share.

You can turn that around by practicing to be lovable. Think and feel love, all the time. You just have to tell yourself often enough, and that will be your way of life, because that is what you are willing, and you only create what you actively will.

Feeling confident is so important, because you cannot release your innate potential until you ask the right question about what makes you tick or what makes your heart sing—until then you will not know what your abilities are, and you will not manifest them.

Being mentally tough is critical to being happy. It starts with being mentally prepared. How you see things is important. Also, most people do very well until something happens that makes them to start slipping backward, with despair and discouragement setting in. This could result from the loss of something important like a job or a partner.

What I am saying is that if you treat such a setback as normal part of life, your mind normalizes it. In that way, it will not overwhelm you, because you are accepting it even though you may not like it. That is a victorious mindset. It encourages your physiology to work on your side. Adrenaline starts thumping your chest. That is a great energy source; it feels good too, and it puts a spring in your step. That uplifted spirit also translates into your brain releasing happy chemicals, like serotonin, oxytocin and dopamine.

A proactive stance makes you mentally tough because you are firm and not reacting to the situation. That leads to more measured responses, which are likely to work better. When you are mentally tough, you tend to be cool too. Keep your attention with you. It is your most precious commodity. Staying cool is a great way to avoid being sucked into a situation of panic, either generated from within or from outside.

Being mentally ready to face challenges is very powerful because you treat setbacks or obstacles with an adventurous spirit. The boost of adrenaline that is liberated charges you up, and you pick up the fight with courage. The adrenaline boost keeps you going! Build a reserve of inner strength, it provides opportunities to keep you going.

To be tough is to be resilient. It means that you have the ability to recover quickly from a setback. So cultivate the qualities of resilience, perseverance, and persistence in order to toughen up.

Of course, having faith in your abilities cannot be overemphasized. You have to know what your strength is. Persistence is what makes you determined to stick it out to the end of a fight or course of action. When you persist, you keep making an effort despite difficulties. This is important because you may have the confidence and boldness to try a course of action, but if you do not have the quality of persistence, then you easily give up. It is important because it makes you keep going forward. Hanging in there for another moment or day may make all the difference. Use the concept of the blueprint that is discussed in later chapters to become a magnet of these three qualities, and your mental toughness will soar.

Act on Your Abilities

This is a crucial step in putting our abilities into action. Positive expectations are very powerful, but they are not enough to give us what we want. Yes, having the conviction that good things will happen sets the motion spiritually, and then things happen, but without action that comes from thinking ahead and planning, nothing will work. The spiritual assets that we have make us feel buoyant, but we have to get past that. What I am saying is that being hopeful is very powerful, but we have to be real too.

Reality is the difference between what we expect, and what *is*. Expectations are powerful, because we rarely go above them, no more than our room temperature goes above the setting on the thermostat.

Look at the Emotional Flow Chart in chapter 1 to appreciate how our actions affect our emotions. I am talking about things like using conscious awareness to smile. Do it often enough and it gets your body going—and your emotions too. More smiling makes your body release happy chemicals.

When people frown, they inspire toxic emotions. Visualize yourself happy. Plant that happy image within. Actively make yourself think that the glass is half full, not half empty. That positively tips your energy balance.

When you force yourself to act this way, you are making use of one of the greatest forces to live by, your thoughts. Your self-image is anchored on them, and your feelings are anchored on self-image.

When you force yourself to make a plan for being happy on a daily basis, you are making one of conscious awareness. That makes you become more motivated from within, and that tends to drive out procrastination. Once you start summoning your body to act, procrastination begins to wither. In a later chapter, you will see how initiating action is going to inspire more action. So initiate feelings of happiness and more good feelings with follow.

How to Release Toxic Emotions

Amanda grew up in a dysfunctional home, so her childhood was less than satisfactory. She had a lot of baggage that held her back. These were things that happened during her childhood that she did not like, like the negative influence for choosing her career. She was still reacting against those negative childhood experiences.

Amanda had therapy sessions with her psychologist, and she reported her progress to me. Toxic emotions are the negative ones like guilt, fear, doubt, anger, and hate. They are toxic because they constitute the spiritual prison cell that we build for ourselves through negative internal dialogue. They are our joy stealers, so avoid them. The best way to avoid them and to avoid being sucked into them is by resisting them. Do not deny negative emotions. How? Do not push them back. Acknowledge whatever you feel. If you feel angry or fearful, acknowledge it. Then let go. Do not dwell on the feeling. When you try to push away negative thoughts, they get repressed into your subconscious mind, which creates a negative self-image that leads to negative feelings. The more you resist, the more you will repeatedly experience the negative or toxic feelings. This is very common in people who play the victim card. They want to give the impression that the problem is out in the world, not them not knowing how to release negative thoughts and feelings.

The reason why it is wrong to resist or deny negative thoughts or feelings is that the mind works by the affirmation principle. This means that it upholds belief, so it can only say yes, not no. This is because the mind is inclusive, not exclusive, so it cannot say no.. So whatever you resist, you attract into your experience.

By using oppositional thinking, you can shift your attention into something else. That will crowd out the negative thought. For example, if you notice feelings of hate coming on, simply think about something lovely. Supplant the negative with anything positive, like a compassionate act of kindness or simply being appreciative of yourself or someone else. This will tip your energy balance forward, which is how you stop the downward spiral.

You can decide today never to resist any situation, because that is what causes a lot of the emotional baggage that people carry with them. Yes, baggage, because it is very heavy. You can feel very light by letting go of negative situations. When you lose something, it is gone. Resisting it is a recipe for getting hurt even more. Let go of it. You can in the midst of the worst crisis, like Amanda experienced, and still be happy. Why? We have to be careful what we believe; in essence, we must choose or filter what we put in our minds. That is how we determine what we experience. Our minds simply translate what we put in, and store it in our subconscious. For example, Amanda has been telling herself over many years that she is inadequate and unworthy. All that became her reality, and that is why she carried the victim mentality and felt so unhappy and emotionally insecure. She stopped feeling like a victim by changing her internal dialogue. She did it by simply believing that the breakup that happened was a path for meeting her dream partner. That act tipped her energy balance positively, and she started moving forward. It is your mind, and you can supplant whatever feels good for you in to it. Yes. You can.

You can see why affirmations are very important. It's because the mind works by the principle of affirmation—it upholds. Amanda had to create a blueprint of core values that she wanted to experience. She then made them into affirmations like, "I feel confident," "I love my life as it is," "I am whole," and "I feel inner peace as I am," and much more. She stood in front of the mirror every evening shortly before falling asleep. She looked herself in the eyes through the mirror. By seeing herself in the mirror and repeating the affirmations to herself, she crystallized the image in her mind of who she wanted to be. She created a solid picture of her self-image that is consistent with the core values of her choosing.

She visualizes herself by standing in front of the mirror. She simply sees herself to be whatever she desires that reinforces the image. She creates affirmations to appreciate herself for all the things that she did right that day, and then releases the things that she did not like. This she did by acknowledging and letting go. By encouraging herself, she feels uplifted. This makes her confidence level soar.

Another part of developing self-confidence comes from the approval that we get from others. The intrinsic source is certainly more powerful than the extrinsic source. But it is important. We feel good about ourselves as our emotions are lifted through appreciation, the external component. I often think that this is more important in children. Giving them encouragement in the form of approval, not telling them what to do, makes them believe more in themselves. For example, if your child wanted to follow a certain career path, you could enlighten him or her by providing education to understand the different options. But do not choose for your child. By doing that, you make his individuality soar, and he is being made responsible to think for himself, which is very important in succeeding. The truth is that only he can summon what he wants with his thoughts. By making that choice, he is also taking responsibility for the eventuality that he may not love the career path later.

How to Develop Broad Feet

The truth is that life is a bumpy ride. In the end, you have to learn how to stand on your own feet. It is also true that we are born as individuals, and are likely to be recycled to the next world alone. So get used to it.

A sense of security is very important. Thinking and feeling that you are worthy and adequate gives you strength. It makes you both psychologically strong and stable. When you exude genuine confidence from within, you do not need to just put on a brave face.

You have to think and feel independent enough to be able to say yes or no without feeling that you owe anybody anything. You really do not. One of the problems that Amanda exhibited in her character was extreme dependency on her partner that she broke up with. It is part of what heralded separation, she confided. She went into it, it seemed, for the wrong reasons. She once said that the main reason that she felt inadequate was because her partner was making all the major decisions for her. That made her feel low. She did not feel fulfilled in the relationship. She felt guilty all the time because she thought that she was not genuine in her relationship. She went into the relationship partly because of the fear of being alone. She did not feel great attraction for her partner. She wanted to be taken care of. This is one of the reasons that she played the victim card. Victimization makes people sympathize, and that is how she gained her attention. It feels good. The problem is that it is short-lived. It does not last long. It is also a way of building a prison cell within, because in order to keep on having sympathy, you have to keep imagining things that will make people feel sorry for you. That perpetuates the negative self-image.

The boundless source of vitality within, our joy of the soul, lasts much longer if we know how to cultivate it. Amanda learned the important principle that having a partner to share his body and possibly material resources would have been a fair motivation had she done it in an empowering fashion—not jumping into a relationship just because she wanted to be taken care of. It created psychological turmoil later on because the thinking was not consistent with her philosophy of life.

To become a magnet for what you want, cultivate the victor's mentality. It is important because spiritual assets can be used to build inner strength. With confidence, people are more likely to be an active agent in their lives, making their own choices and deliberately influencing what is likely to happen.

Lack of confidence is part of why Amanda was so dependent on her partner for making major decisions for her. It took away her individualism, and she did not feel personal fulfillment. She simply followed what her partner decided. She did not make up her mind. She just followed the crowd. That is a dead end.

Victors are also magnets for what they want because they have the gumption to try things without being ravaged by fear of failure. Hence, they are more assertive and adventurous. If it works, it is fine. If it does not work, that's fine too.

Once people entertain the idea that they may lose, they start to feel uneasy, and stress and anxiety ensue. Their bodies get charged with enormous amounts of adrenaline. That is how their sleep gets upset, and such a person may suffer from insomnia. People who are more confident and outgoing tend to be happier.

Fear puts a ceiling on how far you go in life. Being confident and happy enhances your ability to release your innate potential and create success. Why? Because when you are truly confident, you develop your own philosophy and goals that reflect your purpose and set the bar high, forcing yourself to live up to your own standards, not comparing yourself with others. That is stimulating and exciting, a great recipe for making your life interesting. This makes you feel good about yourself and feel more personal fulfillment. There is no better driving force in your life than living your desire and not someone else's.

In order to act on your own terms and have true freedom, you have to think independently. That is how you create the life that you love, and that will give you personal fulfillment.

3. Unleash Your Brainpower

Chapter 3:

Unleash Your Brainpower

"Life is a promise, fulfill it!"

~Mother Teresa

A whole chapter has been dedicated to knowing how the brain works, because it is instrumental in tapping into your boundless source of inner satisfaction. Most of the principles in this book are mediated though the mind. So knowing how to unleash your brainpower is very important.

Many techniques have been described here, but the essence is knowing how to direct or redirect your attention. That is what focusing means, and it is no exaggeration to say that we get what we focus on in life.

To be able to do that is tantamount to having a handle on your life, or control if you wish, that gives personal fulfillment. Why? Interest is the antidote of boredom, and when we are curious about something, we pay attention to it. That raises our level of interest even further. This attention is conscious awareness, so we gain a certain measure of feeling in control, and again our inner satisfaction soars!

So in order to raise your level of inner satisfaction, start paying attention to the details in your life. Part of the puzzle for achieving inner peace is to find wonder in what may seem a mundane or even a dead end job. That magnifies your sense of appreciation and significance; otherwise, life is just going through the motions, which is boring and uninspiring.

When you incorporate excitement and eagerness into your experiences, you raise your level of inner satisfaction.

You will get more interested simply by showing interest in whatever you do. Be curious. Observe the world around you. Boredom comes when the mind wonders, so focus your mind onto something—anything that inspires you and gives you energy or meaning in your life. And if you focus on something that you like or enjoy, it is better. The key is that when you do that you are shifting your attention, which means being in control of your life or your happiness so to speak. Nothing feels better than knowing that you are in control.

Generally speaking, people feel bored and uninterested when they lack something stimulating in their lives.

As for increasing your inner satisfaction, bring your mind to a focused thought or anything interesting. That is how you sustain your attention, and that brings feelings of inner control that translate into inner satisfaction. In life, we only get what we focus on. That is why knowing how to focus is important.

When you force yourself to show interest in something, soon you begin to feel interested in it. Learning, knowing, and doing more about it further inspires more interest and excitement, again, because your attention is sustained in the process.

The same thing applies to raising your level of inner satisfaction. You could start by feeling good about yourself or about anything. The interest that you show stimulates your brain and changes your chemistry. Why is reading so interesting? Because it sustains interest and stimulates the brain as well—well, of course, that is if you love reading. Here is the key: you can only know whether it is interesting by trying it out and applying yourself to it.

It is for this same reason that challenges and adventure feel good, if you have the stomach to digest difficulties—if you are mentally tough.

Being adventuresome changes your chemistry too. The physical movements make your body secrete more endorphins, which make you feel good. Also, your adrenaline shoots up, and when it is harnessed in the right way, it feels good too. You can feel it thumping on your chest.

It is also why doing your work more diligently and lovingly makes it more interesting, as oppose to merely going through the motions. I find that when I listen attentively to my patients, it makes me more interesting and interested. Even if I deal with patients who have similar problems, listening to their stories delicately draws more attention to what I am doing, and that brings more delight to my experience. That magnifies my inner satisfaction, making my life richer and fuller.

The Mind Principle

This principle is very important. It is a must-know, because everything begins with a thought. Simply stated, the mind is like a magnet that draws onto itself whatever we dwell on. That is how thoughts become reality. We think about the thing that we believe, and when held long enough in our consciousness, it becomes our reality. We receive what we believe.

The mind principle is as immutable a law as the law of gravity, because it is present all the time. It cannot simply be turned off, just as we cannot turn off gravity. It acts upon us, whether we know it or not.

This is why our lives follow our thoughts. For the most part, we choose our life by choosing our thoughts. That is, we choose—consciously by using our awareness and unconsciously by default. To influence people, you have to alter their thoughts, actions, or behavior. So knowing how people think and act is important. Decisions are made in the mind, either consciously or unconsciously. It is your greatest gift, so knowing how it works and how to use it is crucial. Psychology is the science of the mind that is concerned with human behavior and personalities.

Why is the mind so important? Because it is everyone's "signature." Conscious awareness precedes most of your actions and behaviors, except those that could be spontaneously mediated by your subconscious mind with very little or no thought. Awareness is important in making a change in behavior or deciding to move forward, as in leadership. This is because your

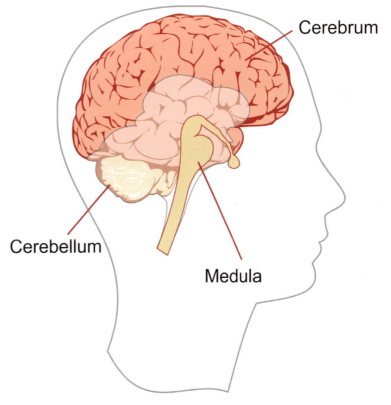

thoughts—all that you experience, real or imagined—are the architect of your life. What you call your truth or reality is created by your thoughts. Everything you are, have, or don't have is in your mind. What you think you own, a house, for example, exists first in your mind. How much value the house is to you, again is in your mind.

The thoughts you harbor form your internal dialogue. This determines how you conceive or interpret the world around you. Your internal dialogue generates your external world too. For example, when someone doesn't like you, it has absolutely no effect on you, unless you try to hate back. Your unforgiving attitude leads to the negative emotions of hate, guilt, and regret. These negative emotions draw psychological pain or suffering into your life. Another way of expressing this is that the negative emotions choke your soul, as you are chained to the past rather than living enthusiastically for today. We are spiritual and imperfect beings, because we all have flaws. This is the rationale for forgiveness—stop resentment against someone. True forgiveness is unconditional like love. It's the ultimate example of love. It's also self-love, because it is very empowering for you. An unforgiving attitude is poisonous for your soul. Your soul is your unconditioned self. It is really who you are. It is eternal. It is wellbeing or joy. It is abundant. It is perfect. On the contrary, your ego is your conditioned self. These are all the attributes, psychological or physical, that are inconsistent with the soul. Things like negative emotions are attributes of the ego. Anything that says that you are lacking is one way or the other, is likely the ego. For example, guilt, unforgivingness, and inadequacy all come from the ego.

Thoughts affect your chemistry too. Having feelings or thoughts that are uplifting releases happy chemicals like serotonin that make you happier too.

I like the story of a man who lived in a very remote area. He had never seen electricity before. This man went to the city to visit a friend. When he saw the many light bulbs shining overhead, he concluded that there were many moons in the city. At first, he thought that he was losing his mind, but he gathered courage and asked his friend, "How come you have so many moons in your city?" His friend made a joke out of him. It took a lot of convincing for him to learn that it was electricity, not the moon; he could only relate to what he knew. Conscious awareness definitely precedes inspired action. Inspired action happens when you line yourself up with your purpose, when you are in harmony. This man could have sat in a dark room, not knowing that all he needed to do to get some light was turn on the switch.

The mind is your thinking faculty. Functionally, it is divided into the conscious and subconscious mind.[1]

You think with your conscious mind, and whatever you habitually think, sinks down into your subconscious mind, which then creates according to the nature of your thoughts. Your subconscious mind is the seat of your emotions. It is the creative mind. If you think good, good will follow. If you think evil, evil will follow. This is because your mind works by affirmation. That is, it upholds whatever you dwell on (good or evil). Your mind can only say yes, it cannot say no. It is inclusive, not exclusive. Once the subconscious mind accepts an idea, it begins to execute it. It works for good and bad ideas alike. It uses the principle of affirmation—it upholds what you believe in. That is, it draws onto you what you think. This is why you attract the experiences in your life that you dwell on.

Your conscious mind is the reasoning mind. This is the phase of your mind that makes choices. You make all of your decisions with your conscious mind, for example, making the choice to live in your home. Your subconscious mind, being the seat of your emotions and memories, feeds your conscious mind with the intuition, based on that past conditioning that where you live now is appropriate.

On the other hand, without any conscious choice on your part, your heart is kept functioning automatically, and the vital functions of all the organs in your body, including your breathing, are carried on by your subconscious mind through the autonomic nervous system, which does not reason things out as your conscious mind does. Your subconscious mind accepts what is impressed upon it or what you consciously believe. The autonomic nervous system links them through reflexes and neurotransmitters.

Positive thoughts, of course, will have a totally opposite effect on you. This is why the positive mental attitude is so powerful. You can reinforce this by using the oppositional thinking. Simply substitute a thought that you do not like with a desired one.

All of your experience and conditioning are produced by your subconscious mind in reaction to your thoughts. Thought is an incipient action. The reaction is response from your subconscious mind that corresponds to the nature of your thought. Thus, thought is an action and your subconscious mind reacts to it.

It is not the things believed in, but the belief itself that brings about the result. Stop accepting false beliefs and fears that may create turmoil in your life. When you feel anxious

---

1 Cecil Andreoli; *Essentials of Medicine*

about an elephant under your bed, whether this assumption is true or false, you get the same reaction. The fight mechanism in your body fires up adrenaline, which gets your heart thumping fast and you begin to feel sweaty. It is not the thing believed in, but the belief in your own mind that brings about the result.

Your subconscious mind does not have the ability to reason like your conscious mind, so it doesn't dispute what it's told. If you're conscious mind gives it information, right or wrong, it will accept it and act on it as if it were true. It will bring your suggestions, even those that are false, to pass as conditions and experiences.

Everything that has happened to you has happened because of thoughts impressed on your subconscious mind through belief. So, repeatedly give your subconscious mind constructive, harmonious thoughts. As these are frequently repeated, your subconscious mind accepts them. In this way, you then form healthy habits of thought and life, because your subconscious mind is the seat of habit.

Get your heroic mission clear and focused. In order to do this, you have to articulate what your end game will look like. You have to imagine, visualize, and see the picture, because only things conceived of the mind can be manifested.

When the picture is clear in your mind, the solutions and the kind of team needed can be put together. You will also be able to seize opportunities when they present themselves.

The statistics are daunting. I have observed that most of one's personal success is rooted from within. This is a direct measure of who you are. This is also the essence of self-leadership. The habitual thinking of your conscious mind establishes deep patterns in your subconscious mind. If your habitual thoughts are peaceful, constructive, and free of fear and worry, your subconscious mind will respond by creating like thoughts. Hence, the importance of selecting thoughts and ideas that inspire, motivate, and fill your soul with joy.

When you get in touch with your basic impulses, visualization is a spontaneous process. The decision-making process happens almost instantaneously. Intuition is often referred to as the sixth sense. This makes problem-solving psychologically complex to explain, but it simplifies the process in a practical manner. Intuition is instinctive insight into the solution of a problem without conscious reasoning—a decision quickly made with little thought involved, even though many factors have an influence on it. The principal element in this behavior is coded in genes.

The Affirmation Technique

To affirm is to verify the existence or truth of a thing. As you maintain this attitude of mind as true, regardless of all evidence to the contrary, you will receive an answer to what your mind perceives as a wish. Your thoughts can only affirm, and so even if you deny something, you are only affirming the presence of what you deny.

The conscious mind is a camera, and the power of your affirmation lies in the intelligent application or specific positives. You affirm good health with the absolute certainty that it is a virtue.

To affirm is to state that it is so. Maintain this attitude of mind as true, regardless of all evidence to the contrary in order to supplant the idea into your subconscious mind—the seat of creation.

Ralph Waldo Emerson, the great nineteenth-century philosopher said, "Do the thing you are afraid to do, and the death of fear is certain." When you affirm positively that you are going to master your fears, and you come to a definite decision in your conscious mind, you release the power of the subconscious, which flows according to the nature of your thoughts.

The mind principle has one mechanism, which is affirmation. Create affirmations based on what you know to be true and on your dreams. Hold whatever you want, positive or negative, long enough in your mind, and it will manifest. This is the universal law of action and reaction.

Constant repetition or rehearsal is important, not only in developing a new habit, but also enhancing memory and learning. The brain easily remembers information when it is constantly challenged or impressed with it.

The Visualization Method

The basis of this technique is the use of imagination. With constant practice, it becomes second nature. If the solution to the problem is not obvious, you toss it into your subconscious mind. Again, choices are made in the conscious mind, which is a camera. The subconscious mind is the film where the picture is cast, where memories are formed.

Everything begins with a thought. Our thoughts are based on our beliefs. We think about what we believe in, and with time, it becomes our reality. That is why we receive what we believe. But in order to create anything, we have to first will it, then visualize or see ourselves doing what we wish to experience. That is how we create the picture within, our self-image. Our external world flows from this picture that we form within—behavior, actions, and feelings. For example, if you wanted to go for a holiday in a hot climate, see yourself sitting there at the beach. This is important because it will help you and encourage you to do what it takes to do it. That fires you up, and you can actually be enjoying a warm climate without even being there.

Similarly, see yourself happy, smiling, talking with confidence and eagerness, and bouncing around with a spring in your step. Your body will pick up these cues, your chemistry will as well, and your feelings will follow.

Simply stated, you replace the thought or the mental movie with one that you wish to experience. A client used this method for quitting smoking. As he explained, he began to imagine the joy of freedom from the smell of smoke. He understands that his conscious mind is like a camera, so he tried to do it as effortlessly as he could. He also imagined his son saying congratulations for quitting. He focused on the scene before him until he gradually identified with the picture that had developed in his mind. He repeated this mental movie frequently in order to have it completely impregnated.

Oppositional Thinking

You want your attention to be on the task at hand, unless it is what you do not want to experience. The essence of this technique is to either help you stay focused or shift attention onto what you wish to experience. Simply put, if you do not like what you are experiencing, change the channel or frequency. That is, shift focus to what you want to experience. Don't try to resist what you don't like. What you resist persists. So, turn on a light for darkness to disappear, don't try to beat darkness. As will be explained in chapter four, you can also use oppositional thinking. It is a very important technique. Simply replace the thought that you do not like with one that you wish to experience.

My client completely believed that he would succeed. This technique has endless applications. For better healing, whatever the ailment is, imagine yourself to be free of it. See your loved ones saying congratulations and feeling good about your healing.

Beware of what you feed your mind with. If your mind is filled up with big and bold ideas, they will energize and motivate you. On the other hand, if your mind is fed with hopelessness and worry, this will lead to tension, anxiety, melancholia, and limitation of all kinds.

When an idea comes to mind that you do not like, acknowledge and accept it, in order for psychological release to happen. When you try to deny it, what happens is that you repress it. What you resist persists.

Guide Your Thinking

The analogy in the Bible is a wonderful way to understand the two functions of your mind. It says that you should think of the mind as a garden. You are the gardener. You are planting seeds of thought in your subconscious mind all day long. These seeds are based on your habitual thinking, so you may not even be aware. As you sow in your subconscious mind, so you shall reap in your body and the world.

Imagine your subconscious mind as a bed of rich soil that will help all kinds of seeds to sprout and grow, whether good or bad. Every thought is a cause, and every condition is an effect. This is why you should take charge of your thoughts. In this way, you can bring forth only desirable conditions.

Entertain all ideas that come to mind and then release them. Do not resist these thoughts because what you resist persists.[2] This is repression, which is very detrimental to your soul and body. You can also use oppositional thinking to substitute for an idea that you do not like. Hence, substitute hate with love.

If you try to resist the word hate, it will persist in your mind. Why? The reason is simple: the mind principle only works by affirmation. You use your conscious mind to choose what you want. So if love is more consistent with your values, when you start thinking of hate, affirm it, and the hate disappears. Affirm love, and hate disappears.

You can start right now to sow thoughts of peace, joy, goodwill, and prosperity. You can do exactly the same thing with the leadership qualities. Think quietly and with conviction on these qualities and principles. Accept them fully in your conscious reasoning mind. Continue to plant these seeds of thought in the garden of your mind and you'll reap accordingly.

Once you begin to control your thought process, you can apply the powers of your subconscious to any problem. This is the world within, which creates the world without. Your thoughts, feelings, and visualized imagery are the organizing principles of your experience. The world within is the creative power. Everything you find in your world of

2 Eugene Braunwald; Harrison's *Manual of Medicine (15th Edition)*

expression has been created by you in the inner world of your mind, whether consciously or unconsciously. If you want to change external conditions, you must change the cause—the way you use your conscious mind, the thoughts and images you entertain. Simply change the cause, and you change the effect.

Once you master how to apply the mind principle skillfully, you will experience abundance instead of poverty, wisdom instead of ignorance, peace instead of strife, success instead of failure, light instead of darkness, and confidence instead of fear. Most successful people and innovators have had a deep understanding of how the conscious and subconscious mind works together. This is what gave them the power to accomplish their dreams.

Your subconscious mind is subject to the conscious mind. That is why it is called subconscious or subjective. In this way, your conscious mind is the one in control. It can tell the subconscious mind what to do. It must obey, because it's subject to its command. It responds to the nature of your thoughts; it's reactive when your conscious mind is full of fear, worry, and anxiety. Negative emotions are created in your subconscious mind. These then flood the conscious mind with a sense of panic and despair. When this happens to you, you can use oppositional thinking to affirm confidence, and your subconscious mind will release the negative emotions.

Your reasoning mind is aware of its environment, either by the senses or intuitively. It is the seat of emotions and storehouse of memories. It performs its highest functions when your objective senses are not functioning. It is this intelligence that makes itself known when the objective mind is suspended or in sleepy, drowsy state. As you think about it, even when you are asleep, all the bodily functions are controlled by this system. You can feed a message into this system, for example, when you want to get up from sleep, and most of the time it works like magic.

Over 90 percent of your mental life is subconscious. If you fail to make use of this great power, you condemn yourself to live within very narrow limits. Your subconscious mind is at work all day long. It maintains all vital functions of the body. It is always trying to help and preserve you from harm. It is in touch with infinite life and boundless wisdom, and its impulses and ideas are always life-preserving. The great aspirations, inspirations, and visions for a nobler life spring from the subconscious, but you can condition and cultivate them through the conscious thoughts that you feed your subconscious. Your most profound convictions are those you cannot argue about rationally because they come from your subconscious, and not from your conscious mind.

Your subconscious speaks to you in intuitions, impulses, urges, and ideas. It is always telling you to transcend, grow, and move forward to greater heights.

Get Results You Desire

To get a complete picture of how the mind works, it's important to know how it controls bodily functions. The interaction of your conscious and subconscious minds requires a similar interaction between the corresponding systems of nerves. The cerebrospinal or voluntary system is the organ of the conscious mind. The autonomic system is the organ of the subconscious mind. The voluntary nervous system is the channel through which you receive conscious perception by means of your physical senses and exercise voluntary control over the movement of your body. This system has its control center in the cerebral cortex of the brain.

The autonomic nervous system has its center of activity in the other parts of the brain, including the cerebellum and the brain stem. These organs have their own connections to the major systems of the body and support their vital functions even when conscious awareness is absent.

The two systems may work separately or in tandem. When a perception of danger arrives at the switching center in the cerebellum, messages are sent both to the conscious and to the subconscious. The person's defensive abilities may start to respond to the danger even before the danger is consciously noted and evaluated.

A client confided in me that the creation of new product line in his organization was the result of his ability to tap the inexhaustible reservoir of his subconscious mind with the task of developing a gimmick for it. Through brainstorming every day, shortly before going to sleep and just after getting out of bed, the whole puzzle on how to market his idea came to him piece by piece.

You can use this great power of your subconscious mind to develop any leadership quality or get any results that you desire. You can do this at any time of the day, but the best time is in the evening when you're going to sleep or shortly after waking up in the morning. Each night, as you go to sleep, enter into a drowsy, meditative state, the condition likened to sleep. Focus your attention on the results or quality desired. What you need to do in order to avoid failure is to accept your idea or request. It responds to your faith or conscious mind acceptance. Feel the reality of your request and be confident about it, and the law of your mind will execute your plan. Turn over your request with faith and confidence, and your subconscious will take over and answer for you.

Lack of confidence and too much effort could lead to failure. So you have to avoid conflict between the conscious and subconscious. Whenever the subconscious mind accepts an idea, it immediately begins to execute it. It uses its infinite resources to that end. It mobilizes all the mental and spiritual laws of your deeper mind. This law is true for both good and bad ideas. Consequently, if you use your subconscious negatively, it brings failure and confusion. When you use it constructively, it brings success and peace of mind.

Decree whatever you want, and stay relaxed, and the all-wise subconscious mind will deliver it to you. Whatever you wish to succeed in—good health, prosperity, or peace of mind—use your imagination, not willpower. Visualize the end, because you have to see what the end will be. Get the feel of the happy ending. The law of attraction has it that this will put you in the creative frequency.

Simply put, in order to stay healthy, picture yourself without the ailment. Then imagine the emotional gratification of the freedom state, without the ailment. Genuinely believe that it is already happening. Don't worry about how it will happen.

Focus your attention on the means to obtain your desire, not on the obstacle. Strive for a harmonious agreement between your conscious and subconscious on the mental image of your desire. When there is no longer any disagreement between the two parts of your mind, your wish will be answered. You can minimize conflict between your wish and imagination by entering into a drowsy state that brings all effort to a minimum. The conscious mind is submerged to a great extent when in a sleepy state. The best time to impregnate your subconscious with a task is just prior to sleep. The reason for this is that the highest degree of outcropping of the subconscious occurs just before going to sleep and just after we awaken. In this state, the negative thoughts and imagery that tend to neutralize your desire and prevent your acceptance by your subconscious mind no longer present themselves. When you imagine the reality of the fulfilled desire and feel the thrill of accomplishment, your subconscious brings about the realization of your desire.

Problem Solving

The greatest skill of all is to learn how to stay focused. This greatly enhances your chance for task-completion. The best way to approach any problem is to use familiar techniques and skills, not by guessing. When you don't have tried and proven methods to apply in problem solving, you can use some of the techniques described in this book, including visualization to have your all-wise subconscious mind to figure out the answer for you. Nothing happens by chance, in either the spiritual or the physical world. There are laws and principles linked together by the universal intelligence that had neither time nor space.

This is a great problem-solver. You can use this technique in any walk of life, medicine or research, business or personal. Simply ask the "what are the options" question, and let your mind wander. It stimulates the brain and unlocks its creativity and genius, especially when a pressing problem is at hand. When faced with great pressure or pushed out of your comfort zone, adrenaline shuts off. You go into the deep and all-wise subconscious and come up with interesting solutions for your problem.

This technique clarifies your vision. Once you lay out the different options, you can see the big picture.

Author and businessman, Charles Haanel, in his master key system, suggests that this technique works best when you do it in writing.[3] It stimulates the brain to be more creative.

So, get a piece of paper. Write down as many options as possible to solving a problem.

I use this method in my practice with great success. I know that the door for change in people's lives swings outward. Also, people have the bigger picture of what is happening to their lives, if only they could think-act-feel to make a difference. They are the only ones who can change their mental state. I only listen to see if I can redirect them to something they may be overlooking, or to sympathize or empathize, but the solution is ultimately in their hands. Quite often, in complex issues, I hand the pen and paper to them, give them time to brainstorm, and instruct them on how to use the technique. I'm quite impressed at the solutions that most people can bring up for a seemingly complicated problem.

---

3 Charles Haanel; *The Master Key System*

The Magnet

To be a magnet is to draw onto yourself what you desire, not chase it. This is consistent with how the mind works. So, in order to possess the quality of confidence, you start by thinking, acting, and feeling confident. For example, if you want to be loved, you have to be lovable, and this you do by thinking, acting, and feeling as though you love. So simply put, create a blueprint for any quality that you wish to develop and practice to great effect until it becomes second nature.

Calmly think over what you want, and visualize its coming to fruition from this moment forward. Again, use no effort. This is because your conscious mind is like a camera. Do not try to push too hard, just present the idea as a brief affirmation, a simple phrase. The subconscious mind is like the film, which develops or releases the idea that becomes a reality or a full picture.

There is always a direct response from the infinite intelligence of your subconscious mind to your conscious thinking. The fundamental and most far-reaching activity in life is that which you build into your mentality every waking hour. Your thought is silent and invisible, but it is real. Your thoughts represent your life story, your identity, your personality, or whatever you wish to create.

Moment by moment, you can build success by the thoughts you think, the beliefs you accept, and the scenes you rehearse in your mind. Act as though you are, and you will be.

Buddha observed that what we are is a result of our thoughts. Our thoughts are the cause, and our external world is the effect.

You must ask believing that you are to receive. Your mind moves from the thought to the thing. You must reach the point of acceptance in your mind, an undisputed state of agreement. This contemplation should be accompanied by the feeling of joy and assurance of the accomplishment of your desire.

By redirecting your conscious mind to dwell upon virtues rather than vices, your subconscious mind will accept your blueprint and bring all of these things to pass.

So why, is one person a success and another is a failure? Most of the answer is in the fact that one of them learned how to use his most precious possession, his mind, and the other did not. What you truly believe in and feel strongly about, you now know how to fill up your mind with until you begin to overflow. That is how you become a magnet of your desires. You are a magnet full of energy, ideas, ambition, and confidence. You come to the realization that life belongs to the bold and meek. You start to think like a winner. Losers, on the contrary, don't believe in themselves, they exercise false humility. They are so timid that any bold move is perceived as arrogance. Consequently, they are melancholic perfectionists, energetically flat, full of fears, cynicism, and doubt.

I cannot stress enough how important using your mind is. It's the great master that you should know how to exploit. The foundation for everything in your life, spiritual or physical, is laid in this storehouse. It's a small wonder that when it's gone, you're finished too. Your world is simply your mirror—but where is the mirror? It is the words you use and the behavior actions that are deemed yours; the character and personality that are ascribed to you emanate from this storehouse.

As a physician, I know immediately that I am dealing with an autistic child, just from the way he relates, his mannerisms, or how he behaves.

A positive mental attitude goes hand in hand with optimism and hope. It is imagining and expecting the best, but at the same time, accepting and preparing for the worst-case scenario. It frees up wasted energy on worrying or brooding about the past or things that don't come to fruition. Positive thoughts are buoyant and uplifting as opposed to negative thoughts that sap one's energy.

A positive mental attitude can transcend any situation. No matter how badly you have been treated, if you genuinely decide to let go and move forward, you will. It is a great psychological release. It frees up the wasted energy that holds you back when you resist a situation.

4. Develop a Sense of Purpose

Chapter 4:

Develop a Sense of Purpose

"Knowing 'why' is crucial to achieving anything."

- Anonymous

Mr. McAvoy came to see me with one of his daughters, Deanna. In his words, his daughter was the most pleasant person in the world. She had all the features of a brilliant, beautiful girl. His main frustration with her was that she was lazy. She put off doing her school projects until she was "in the mood."

Deanna had repeated interviews with me, which revealed that she was a procrastinator. She was immature for her age and had very low frustration tolerance. She sat and waited until the last few days of her school project, and then zoomed around the house driving everybody bonkers. And when she finally got to it, she did it with a very carefree and casual attitude. She did not take pride in her work.

She did not think of her work in a positive way. She saw it as kind of a yoke on her neck that prevented her from having a joyous life—an impediment to expand and evolve rather than the path for joy and dignity that work brings.

I gave her an earful of practical advice and exercises to do in order to crank her up. She improved magnificently.

A sense of purpose is the main reason behind what draws us to action. When you are not sure why you are doing what you're doing, simply ask the question: Why? This stimulates your thinking, to get you connected with your inner purpose, your impulses, and instincts, so you can intuitively see your desire for the action clearly. William James, one of the early American psychologists, observed that actions follow thoughts and feelings follow actions.

Seeing your purpose clearly ahead of you, initiates the positive thoughts, which together with the positive feelings that follow, coalesce into an action.

This is why ambition and motivation are crucial forces in self-improvement. There has to be a rationale for your action, otherwise why not sit quietly and just savor the moment rather than get involved in gainless activity.

You can see why all action in the universe has two reasons: to gain pleasure or move away from pain.

Deanna has the chance of escaping her mother's wrath if she does her school project in a timely fashion. She will also benefit from the positive emotion of fulfillment as she contemplates the finishing of the project, or when she finishes the project. The feeling of satisfaction that comes with a job well done.

This feeling of satisfaction is the basis of life, because as humans we are made to thrive with joy and dignity. It's a primal right for us—to be joyous and have well-being.

In terms of doing things, there is ample evidence that you have to prime the pump by getting started, whether you feel like it or not.

The next time when you have a project, force yourself to begin work on it. Once you get started, it will encourage you to do even more. When the ball gets rolling, that little bit of action builds a momentum that grows.

The diagram below illustrates how action can lead to motivation, and then to further action.

The more you do, the more you feel like doing, but doing sometimes comes first.

I have talked about confidence, and how crucial it is in success, but successful people do not always feel confident. They sometimes endure bouts of their own frustration, fear of failure.

They use different strategies, well-developed coping skills like patience, discipline, and persistence to help them stay afloat.

Achieving one's personal goals can be challenging and stressful too. You will often have to overcome numerous obstacles and setbacks along the way.

This is crucial in the art of succeeding in life, because if you think that life is easy and that you don't have to struggle, you may conclude that a particular task is too difficult and give up when things get tough.

To be highly successful, you have to know that there will be normal rejections, frustrations, and failures. Everybody understands that harm and pain are a part of life.

People, in an attempt to look good, will not tell you all of what it takes to achieve what they have. Even building your character and values takes lots of effort. It sometimes involves trial and error through personal experience. Learn from your experience and from the experience of others. These are the only two ways you can experience something. We all have winner wisdom if we choose to use it. Through imagination you can experience something that has not happened to you or others. But the commonest way to experience something is when it happens to you—learn from mistakes, both your own and those of other people.

Smart people can learn from things that happen to somebody else. In this way you do not have to endure it.

When you encounter adversity, you simply say that yes, things are the way they should be. That tough-mindedness makes you persist, and when you do, you prevail.

Challenges become building blocks of monuments; as others put them on your path you become Mr. or Mrs. Glass-Is-Half-Full. You see opportunity, not failure. You see hope, not despair. You see optimism, not pessimism.

Challenges take a totally different flavor for you, because they begin to feel good. That's why adventurous people enjoy life more. It's the ride that gives you the shot of adrenaline that keeps you going.

You become a go-getter. You feel no frustration when you fail, because you have a very high frustration tolerance; so disappointments don't mean anything to you. Your attention is the only thing you have, so by so doing, you are investing it into a worthy endeavor, rather than wasting it on a past failure.

You become so dynamic that, after failure even in a test or business deal, you do not waste time dwelling on it. Immediately, you start planning for your next test or business deal, leaving the failure behind you, making a renewed commitment, with determination to move on.

You can apply this important principle to any subject, in your studies or relationships.

Sometimes the person you are pouring all of your energy into is simply not meant for you; in a very positive sense, you relax, feel the disappointment for a while, and let go. Review what you have learned so far on how to release negative feelings or experiences.

When it comes to hard work, there's a saying, "Do not feed the chicken on the day you are going to sell it." What this means is that the chicken will not suddenly grow in one day, and that the effort you put into feeding the chicken long before the market day, perhaps many months before the day of selling it, is more important.

So adopt hard work as a core value for success but hard work goes together with discipline. It is discipline that gets you out of bed early in the morning. It is discipline that makes you ignore the weather and just go for the hike even though it's wet outside. I say this because the basis of discipline is willpower.

Understand, therefore, that you may need to put a totally different level of effort and time to achieve the results you desire. Every day ask yourself what you can do to progress in the direction of your goal, joy!

Achieving your goals makes you feel good about yourself; then you want to do more, and then you do better, and better. That's how you achieve excellence. This is called the positive emotion of fulfillment.

This feeling of fulfillment or satisfaction is a very important motivating force in your life. If you feel good about your effort, it will motivate you to work harder. Take pride in your work! Don't just go through the motions. Do it with zeal and gusto—as if you love it. That's how you get adrenaline flowing in your body: through action. And you feel great about yourself as you watch the magic happening in your life.

When it comes to living your purpose, I like the analogy of a dynamo, the device for converting mechanical energy into electrical energy. This is because living without a purpose is like having a dynamo that is not connected to a lightbulb to deliver light, so the energy in the dynamo is not harnessed, it is wasted. The key here is to align your goals with a wider purpose; otherwise, you just waste your energy.

Your purpose is the big picture or the thread that holds everything together. Your purpose, or what some people call their dream, transcends your goals. Goals are the steps that you take in order to achieve your purpose. A goal therefore, is an ongoing pursuit of your working purpose until accomplished. Goals help you focus. Why? When it comes to goals, I like the analogy of the soccer match because I am a coach. Imagine a soccer match without a goal post. What a waste of time! There would be no focus or meaning in the whole process. Not having a goal post would result in dribbling aimlessly all over the field. Then what? No excitement. Remember the excitement that people show when a goal is scored. And the wider purpose that makes people feel exhilarated because it resonates with their personal philosophy, hence giving them significance.

When I was starting a micro-financing company in West Africa, my wider purpose was to relieve poverty. That gives me meaning in what I am doing, because I truly feel that I am making a difference in other people's lives. That sense of purpose makes me feel good about my action.

The key question to get to your calling is why you do whatever you're doing. The point is, if not anything you do makes a difference, why do it? You want to feel that you matter or that you are making a difference on the planet.

Self-improvement is an important aspect of guiding yourself in order to succeed. The reason is that you have to be able to lead yourself or others who are involved in whatever area of success that you desire.

Leading is simply the process of helping yourself or others get somewhere. This is important because ultimately you have to be able to take care of yourself, before you try to care for others. You have to be able to deal with challenges by yourself or bring in other people or resources to assist you. You are a creative individual, so you should be able to make your own judgment and decisions.

The essence of living our dream is finding out what our strength is and then living it. Different people go about it differently, but the simplest thing to do is ask yourself what makes your heart sing.

Ideally, lining up yourself with your purpose is priceless, but living in such harmony is but a dream for some people. Should that be the case, they should still try to love their job even though they may not like it. It is possible using the mind principle. How?

According to the mind principle, it is not the thing believed in but the belief itself that brings about results. This explains why two people may do the same job, and although one loves it, the other person may not like it. Review what you have learned so far on how the mind works, and this becomes clearer.

What I am describing is a perspective that not everybody will fit into the mold. It is conceivable that there are people who are so gifted that they have more than a few things that they enjoy doing and that there are going to be people who have outside interests that are different from their day job.

A sense of purpose makes you feel good about yourself and is uplifting. This is the feeling of fulfillment.

How you react to situations depends on your personal philosophy, values, and worldview. Consequently, the information that two billion people live on less than two dollars a day may mean different things to different people. This explains why so many people die of hunger each day.

I always see philanthropy as my calling—poverty relief is a critical part of it. I want to be the king of philanthropy. I am ready to do anything in my capacity to champion any global initiative aimed at relieving poverty. It is no secret that feeding the hungry and getting people, especially those without the financial means, to be educated are all measures to relieve poverty. There is a very direct correlation between lack of education and poverty.

Part of my worldview is that anyone anywhere in the world should have food on the table; it's a basic necessity. In the twenty-first century, people should not die of hunger or go to school hungry.

The greatest hurdle is in realizing our dream. I find that people want to start big. But the key is to start a positive step. You have to start moving forward in the right direction. Indeed making small incremental steps each day, like termites gnawing on the root of the tree, is a great secret for success. In the end the termites are wiser, as their seemingly miniature bites fell a big tree.

My observation, and that of people I trust in self-improvement and self-motivation, is that a small step taken now is far more important than a giant step anticipated later. The only derailment here is only if the timing is not right—otherwise, why wait?

Simply identify a niche where there is need for something that you are passionate about, like poverty for me. Whatever I do, so long as it's meant to relieve poverty, it lights up my heart. It means that I feel fulfilled, and as my adrenaline is flowing, I feel energetic and find that I am acting on purpose.

Always keep in mind what your purpose is. If a person has a list of the goals he wants to achieve sitting on his table, he sees them as often as possible. This enables him to supplant his goals into his subconscious mind, to connect with his basic impulses. I constantly counsel people to visualize their dream life on a daily basis. You simply close your eyes and see your goals complete. This is best done shortly before you go to bed or shortly after getting out of bed in the morning. But any time of the day is good.

If feeding the hungry was your goal, simply see the picture of somebody having a warm meal in your mind's eye. You do not have to prostitute your dream. You can live it very quietly, leaving footprints in a very positive way. I always say that you should let others perceive and see their world the way they want it to be. There is a lot of need in the world. What we lack are people prepared to take up these needs as causes to adopt as part of their lives. Do not force people to live the same dream as you. Again, the information here is not meant to tell you what to think; it is here to help you think through the different steps in order to create and live a dream of your choice.

The principles outlined here are therefore guidelines on how to face challenges and how to think through problems when they present themselves.

5. See Yourself Happy

Chapter 5:

See Yourself Happy

"In the depth of winter I finally learned that there was in me an invincible summer."
~Albert Camus, *Lyrical and Critical Essays*

Joel came in with his mother to see me because he had no time to do anything. He was failing his grades. He was not sure what to do. According to his mother, he used foul language and was ignorant about the consequences of his actions. She thought that Joel was just confused about how to approach his life. He slept in until eleven o'clock in the morning on weekends. He had not been happy since he started failing his classes. He used to be a very happy kid.

I asked Joel on what he thought about all the things that his mother talked about. He just stared, and we sat there silent for ten minutes with no answer, so I gave him a piece of paper and pen to brainstorm. I asked him to write down what his goals and values were.

He wrote more than ten different things, but they weren't great or dreamy. The tone of his words was negative and cynical. It was all about his mother forcing him to do this or that, all against his will and better judgment.

Joel wasted his time fighting the negative people in his life. These were his words. He was always at war with everybody. He always had something negative to say about every subject.

I found out that Joel was a very smart kid. He was smart enough to try to steer away from the negative crowds, with their potentially negative influences on him. His problem was that he did not know how to do it. He instead attracted all the negative people into his life. That is what drew so much pain into his life.

When I first saw Joel, he was as stiff as a coiled wire. He did not speak with eagerness and enthusiasm.

Every word that came out of his mouth was about something wrong about somebody else. In essence, he had a very negative attitude, and he was not focusing on what mattered to him.

I have had a lot of inspiration from Esther and Jerry Hicks, authors of *Ask and it is Given*, regarding how to focus in your life. They think that the greatest skill of your life is to know how to direct your thoughts toward your dreams.[4] They assert that to get to what you really want, ask yourself why you are doing whatever it is you're doing. This moves your energy to the solution, rather than focusing on the problem.

Joel did just the opposite of that, he was sapping his energy by focusing on negative people rather than directing his thoughts to what he wanted to accomplish, either for the day or for his life.

In order to do this, you have to stop the negative thoughts—sometimes you may need to use a mirror exercise for releasing negative experiences. To do this, place yourself in front of a mirror, and look at yourself in the eyes. If there are any negative thoughts and feelings in your mind, first acknowledge them. The use of affirmations that speak to what you desire can also be done. They tend to crowd out what you do not like. To affirm is to simply state that it is. It is similar to bringing the light in the presence of darkness, as the darkness simply disappears. When you affirm, you are shining the light of conscious awareness, which dissolves the negative thoughts or ignorance that tends to incubate the toxic emotions of fear, doubt, guilt, and more.

The use of affirmations is consistent with how the mind works by upholding what you profess. Seeing yourself in the light of your desire creates and reinforces the picture within—your self-image.

The affirmations could relate to things that happen that same day or anything that you want to supplant into your subconscious mind. Simply, create the blueprint for the quality or desired experience, and practice it over and over for great effect. Repetition is important because you need about twenty-one days to form or change a habit.

Why is this important? Our image is the anchor of our emotions. But our image flows from our thoughts. So in order to create the desired picture within that generates our behaviors, actions, and feelings, we first have to change our internal dialogue from negative to positive. That then changes our negative picture to a positive one.

Always move your thoughts toward what you wish to experience. What do you really desire?

---

4 Esther and Jerry Hicks; *Ask and It Is Given*

Give attention to good-feeling thoughts. Focus on what feels good. Esther and Jerry Hicks think that when you do this, you start to experience the positive emotion of relief.[5] Joel was given positive affirmations to repeat to himself shortly before falling asleep. The mirror exercise was also crucial here. I instructed him to look for the things that went well during the day and repeat them to himself, and to simply ignore the negative people that he worried so much about. That was redirecting his attention to the worthy, which was putting him in control of himself.

According to Esther and Jerry Hicks, just shortly after waking up in the morning, is a good time to practice positive affirmations, because during sleep you are detached from your negative vibrations. Thus, it's easier to align your energies or get into harmony with the core of who you are—your wellbeing.

The positive thoughts, by the law of attraction, will draw like thoughts as the rest of your day unfolds. The law of attraction simply asserts that you get what you focus on.

Success or failure in your life has to do with your attitude for the most part. The way you react to anything has more to do with your attitude than the facts. The choices you make depend on that as well. Your life is simply a series of choices. Why? Because exploring the options, and making choices, is your main leverage in life for dealing with any situation. It is very difficult to change people or circumstances.

The reason that I emphasize thoughts is because they are the main factor that we can change in our life. At the time I am writing this book, an earthquake happened in Haiti. The more I observe the problems that they are facing now, the more I realize how unfair life could be. What have they done to deserve this? Thousands of people were killed by the earthquake, and they were dumped into mass graves! I can find an uncountable number of examples where the obstacles are simply beyond our control. In these circumstances, we accept them once we face the challenge and use the resources within our realm of options and capacity to no avail. Until that happens and we create a new blueprint that takes our focus from the apparent problem, or earthquake in this situation, we cannot move forward. The earthquake becomes baggage as we stick to it as we are trying to resist it.

This is why your attitude is important. It's the way you think and behave. But the language and the tone of the delivery comes from how you think too. Your values determine what your belief or truth is. Truth is a perspective you have depending on what you

---

5 Esther and Jerry Hicks; *Ask and It Is Given*

believe in. Because when you think about what you believe long enough, it becomes your reality.

Pay attention each time, not to the details, but to the context of the moment. Shift your attention to where the heart of the moment requires. That is how you order your life. Otherwise, you diminish your energy. Days disappear without any significant accomplishment.

Do not be stuck on details—only important details matter in life. The big picture is always more important than the details. Simply say what the issue is and the context. Until you understand the context, you will not wear the hat that the moment requires. To do that is to be in control of yourself; you are directing, and redirecting your attention, every moment, onto what you desire to experience. You get what you focus on, from both a spiritual and material sense. We think all the time about what we believe in, and when that happens over the long haul, it becomes your reality. No wonder that we receive what we believe.

There is no question that what we believe is limited to a degree by reality. Because reality is the difference between what we expect and what is. The point about belief is simply that we will hardly go above what we expect. Underscore the importance of thought and belief, because our life follows them!

The context becomes your dominant force for that moment. For example, you have affirmations to recite in bed, but even more important is your primary focus, going to sleep, so the dominant thought is sleep, sleep, sleep, and you relax and fall asleep.

Always use the thermostat to change the temperature of the room at will. You can also at will focus on only the positive things and on the thoughts that feel good. You want to be in harmony with who you are—your soul—it feels good!

No matter how dire a situation is, you can always find something positive. The best way to do this is to think, not of what you are seeing, but what you imagine could be. That kind of creativity opens doors or possibilities, because being creative is being full of ideas. That kind of big-picture thinking, which makes us see beyond our personal needs, is very empowering. Thinking small tends to stifle our creativity because we are in a "straight jacket" or comfort zone. We can only find the silver lining (something positive), by redirecting our attention to it.

To cultivate a positive internal dialogue, which is a precursor to a positive self-image, we have to consciously dwell on what is positive. It is not that we do not know that someone rubbed us the wrong way. We do know; but the key to maintaining our inner satisfaction is to choose not to dwell on that mishap. Instead, we must shift our attention onto what we wish to experience, staying on the bright side of things.

The universe has limitless options; it's the principle of abundance. There are endless possibilities and the universe can deliver whatever you desire!

Thoughts are the thermostat, for you cannot go higher than your thoughts. It's also fair to say that you cannot exceed your expectations.

Thoughts are very powerful; the key is choosing the right thoughts. And your expectations or dreams determine what kind of thoughts you think. That is how your goals help you focus.

This is why your level of expectation is important; you simply cannot shoot a target that you do not see clearly. So, setting forth an intention of where you want to be and putting your attention on it is crucial.

It's fair to say that your thinking meets you at your level of expectancy.

This is a simple but important concept, for example, optimists expect the best, and pessimists expect the worst.

Your attitude is the key to anything you want to be, do, or become. Attitude is the way you think and behave. The words that come out of your mouth are a result of your internal dialogue.

The most powerful skill you can ever learn, according to Esther and Jerry Hicks, is how to direct your thoughts to what you want.

Many psychologists have said that attitudes are more powerful than facts. As you think about it, anything we own physically we first own through our thoughts.

In any number of stories of people facing the same dire circumstances, one of them beats the odds, prevails, and is happy, and the other person feels so disappointed about the situation that he takes even his own life.. When I conducted the interviews for my survey, I saw many people faced with the same circumstances looking at them in very different ways. The people who focused on the bright side of things were inevitably happier than those who wallowed in self-pity.

Your spirit is your dynamo or your powerhouse, as I have already said. But to use it, you have to do so through your thoughts. This is why your thoughts are so crucial.

I have also talked about how happiness or a feeling of joy is the path through which you release your potential. Again, this is because feeling good is your creative frequency. You cannot get into harmony with the powerhouse otherwise. The state of joy is compatible or in harmony with the core of your being. And negative feelings are incompatible with your spirit.

Esther and Jerry Hicks assert that in order to allow this natural state of well-being to flow into your experience, you have to focus on what feels good or what you want.

It is sensible because when you feel uplifted, your brain will release happy chemicals, like serotonin, which tends to make you feel happier. Consequently, focusing on either lack, or the things that you do not want or like, will create psychological resistance, hence, blocking the flow of well-being.

Let your thoughts match your bigger perspective. Raise your expectations by focusing your thoughts to your intentions, which should be your dreams or goals.

This should be the essence of your values—the things that put a smile on your face.

It's your thoughts that create. Thoughts that are connected to your broader perspective are inspired thoughts. They arc highly effective because they lead to inspired actions too. To achieve that is to live in harmony, and that feels good.

From a spiritual perspective, psychological resistance comes from negative emotions. You have seen the genesis of negative emotions, as Esther and Jerry Hicks explain; it's resistance to your natural state of well-being. In other words, negative emotions encumber or resist the flow of your natural well-being.

The point is that negative emotions draw psychological pain or resistance onto you. That's what suffering entails—it's through your mind that you suffer psychologically.

To avoid such pain, stop resisting anything that you do not like. You can see why I advised the fellow who was trying to fight negative people in his life, to simply ignore them. The reason is that the more he tried to push them away, the more pain he drew to himself. In a psychological way he did. The more he pushed, the more intense were the negative emotions he attracted to himself. It further destabilized him and pushed him off-balance.

Like a magnet, you draw what you think about into your life.

Feeling good will activate the powerhouse or dynamo, which is your spirit or the core of your natural well-being. This is why good-feeling thoughts are important—because they help you enter into harmony with the essence of who you are. That is what leads to inspired actions; otherwise, a lot of your effort will be sterile because it's aimless. Again, inspired actions feel good, as they are in harmony with your wider purpose.

You can see that only the thoughts that feel good and are directed toward your desire are productive. That is how you harness the energy from your dynamo—otherwise it's dissipated.

That is how many people waste their time and energy. They think and talk about things that they do not like. What a waste of time. They practice false humility, which is their worst characteristic. The problem with this mentally is that when confronted by almost anything you think of doing, they view it as being too ambitious. The reason is that they shoot into the gutter rather than pointing up in the sky where the stars are. They call it humility. No, it's simply timidity, which is a terrible illness of the mind. People who are truly humble, think about other people's needs and help them. That is the true meaning of humility. They are difference makers because they are not self-centered. They also possess the quality of being proactive. So they focus on solving problems, not worrying about problems as those with false humility do. This is important because people who are truly humble, do not worry about themselves or other issues because they are stimulated and engaged in doing things. And the motion of their actions makes their bodies release adrenaline and happy chemicals like endorphins. This is why action and motion feel good. I have observed that people who are active are often happier than those who spend their whole day watching television.

You pity these people because of their false humility; they pretend to make everybody happy.

People you feel you have to try to please, are people who can never be pleased; while others you try to please will tell you that you do not have to. Do good things for people for a larger perspective of abundance, because it feels good. Abundant mentality is the feeling that there is enough to go around, as opposed to the scarcity mentality. It is spiritually powerful because it makes you see opportunity. When you think lack, your mind sees impossibility, rather than possibility, and that limits you spiritually, psychologically, and physically. Giving is receiving and loving. The message here is that only you can make yourself happy. Nothing else, nobody else, can make you happy. Happiness is a choice that you make. Once you make that decision, you need to do the inner work that is required; it's not a gift. Why? Because we all have the soul-source. We just have to learn how to harness it.

Your thoughts also affect your emotions. William James is one of the early psychologists who demonstrated that "we weep because we started thinking sorrowful thoughts."

Your experience or life follows your thoughts. Doesn't the temperature at home follow the thermostat? And your thoughts are like a thermostat, you cannot perform better than your thoughts, unless through miracles, but in the same breath I'd say that's not a smart way to order your life. It is important to be hopeful, but that's not enough, you need a plan and action.

From today, know then that your thoughts are very instrumental in releasing and living your potential. Your thoughts are the medium through which the release is done. I look at your brain as the hardware, and your soul as the software; you need both for optimal realization of joy.

People feel depressed because they first think discouraging thoughts. The feeling of disappointment and regret ensues. The attraction of more of these negative thoughts reaches a crescendo—depression

If you often think thoughts that are positive and joyful, you're going to benefit through creation of positive emotions. That's how you become happy.

So to feel good, you start by feeling good. You can see that if you spend the whole day smiling without good-feeling thoughts that you are directing to your goals, you will not achieve anything. A sense of purpose is an important part of this equation. It helps to motivate you as well. Positive stimulating thoughts are great, but without combining with inspired action, they will avail to nothing. They are the seat of judgment that is a crucial part of your decision-making. The words you speak, and how you speak them, also come from there.

There is no better way to achieve this than through your behavior. Whatever you are, become, or do, you radiate electromagnetic vibrations. Your actions are the loudest noise you can ever make.

Everything in life is a pyramid, observed Jim Rohn, author and motivational speaker. Thus some people will choose to move ahead. Some will choose to stay where they are.

Sometimes there are no reasons. Some will choose to cry; there is nothing wrong with crying.

The point is to let them be. This is because only they have the power to change their attitude or desire. Only they can summon their own desires, through their thoughts and feelings, to experience lives that are worthy.

Here is your transformation. Focus on the positive. Shift your attention to what you want to experience and all else disappears. With this mindset, you can transcend any negative situation, irrespective of the facts, and still prevail.

6. Freedom from Toxic Emotions

Chapter 6:

Freedom from Toxic Emotions

"Being in a relationship purely because it makes you happy may leave
you more vulnerable to disappointment than one in which you also share
common values or one in which you can make yourself happy."

~*Schopenhauer*

In her school, Melisa is nicknamed the "drama queen." Her attitude in dating is of the essence. She can make her point very easily and clearly.

Melisa's father, Mr. Brown, confided in me that he lost count of how many dates she had within one year. One psychologist told him that Melisa has histrionic personality disorder, but he did not know what that meant.

Melisa is on the phone in her room in the evenings. The phone rings constantly at home. He hears deep voices on the phone, but Melisa says they are girls. Her grades are also failing.

She stays in her room for days after a breakup with a boy. She sometimes tries to hide it from her parents, but the signs are there—red eyes after long periods of withdrawal in her room.

"We, as a family, have offered support for her, but she refuses it. We have told her that it's not good to hold on to negative feelings. She will do herself a great favor by just letting out those feelings. And, even more important, have a straight talk with us. It's good for her to be open with us. Staying inside the closet is not the way to get help."

Pathologic lying is one of the big issues with Melisa. Mr. Brown found condoms in her purse, but she denies even knowing what they look like.

"Well," I interrupted, "give her the benefit of the doubt. Maybe she is involved in a sex education club and is scared to tell you because you may jump to conclusions. Let's listen to her side of the story."

Melisa's father seemed very doctrinaire, eager to get the "cold facts" from Melisa to name names about who she was doing what with.

"Tell him, Melisa," he instructed, in an almost deafening tone of voice. Melisa looked at me as if she were saying, "Help me, please, get me out of this mess!"

I charged in. "Well, if you are interested in 'squeezing out' the truth from people, I'd suggest that you go and work at Guantanamo Bay in Cuba. I should inform you though, that tactic doesn't work."

"We learn how to 'massage the truth' from our clients, still leaving them with their dignity and freedom."

Melisa sat for more than ten minutes without saying anything. Finally, I had to bring her back for another session. Melisa took lots of material home to study regarding love, relationships, and dating.

Your key to loving or being loved is in your self-image. This is simply because you perceive the world as you conceive yourself to be.

To love is to accept unconditionally. Self-love is unconditional self-acceptance. It begins with thoughts of acceptance—positive internal dialogue. A positive self-image then results within.

To accept yourself, as you are, means that you see yourself as being whole, lacking nothing. That is important because what we see in the external world is a projection of the picture that we have within. That is how we radiate love. It is also how we become loveable. Think about what you have learned in this book on becoming a magnet of whatever you desire.

We become a magnet or channel of love by thinking lovely thoughts that create a picture within. We then radiate love as we speak, act, and feel. It comes out in our behaviors, in tone of voice, and the language that we use with self or others.

We radiate exactly what we have within, Simply duplicating the picture that we have within to the external world.

When we feel great within, we orchestrate a positive drag, drawing people to the top of the mountain with us. The excitement that we feel comes out in good ways like acts of kindness, unconditional giving of self or material, and encouraging and uplifting others.

On the other hand, people feel hateful because they entertain hateful thoughts. The negative internal dialogue leads to a negative self-image. It is no wonder that toxic emotions like anger, hate, and fear ensue. The lack of self-acceptance leads to feelings of inadequacy and a feeling of being empty. These people feel like they are inside a hole. They project this very negative self-image to their external world. Negative drag is initiated in order to draw others into the hole with them.

The best way to stop slipping into the same hole is to deny being dragged into it. Refuse to be reactive to a negative situation; because if you do, you are easily drawn into the web. That is how you attract toxic emotions onto yourself. That is how you draw psychological suffering onto yourself.

If you cultivate the key positive emotions of excitement, love, and hope, as explained under how to become a magnet, then you are being proactive. Once you are filled with these great positive emotions, they will crowd out the toxic emotions automatically. You will enjoy these great positive emotions, so much so that you will not see the need to descend from your top of the mountain and join misery in the valley.

If you can achieve that, you'll gain a great measure of self-control in the sense that you are learning how to think, will, and create what you want, and not be sucked into someone else's mold. To gain control of yourself is a sure-fire path for personal fulfillment. Be disciplined to be a retailer of love, hope, and excitement, and not hate; hopelessness, and boredom. The former are the building blocks of inner satisfaction, the latter are recipe for a spiritual prison cell.

Positive internal dialogue about self and others makes it easy to feel loving. Feelings follow thoughts. In the beginning, it starts as an idea, which grows into a thought and forms the positive emotion of love.

At that time, you have become familiar with the idea and it becomes a belief. "I believe that he loves me." So feelings of love become more intensified as you think more about him. Soon it becomes, "I feel loved, so I am loved. Now it's a fact: he loves me."

You could now say, "I am in love," as you feel the exhilaration. That's how you become a magnet for love. To be loved, you have to be lovable.

I explained that in relationships, especially during the period of novelty when the positive feelings are most intense, you are willing to go along with your partner. In that mindset, you look for what you want to see in your partner. And since you only see what you look for, you will see what you want. This makes the positive feelings more intense. So you begin to feel in love, "I love him." At this time, there is great peace within. You are lined up with your soul. All the internal conflict within you is dissolved. You feel euphoric, energetic, enthusiastic, confident, and full of ideas.

Sometimes relationships fail – either for reasons that could be avoided or because it is not the right relationship and this new skill set keeps you aware of your mental health and wellbeing in time to get out of it. The interest wanes and waxes with periods of boredom. Emotions are cyclical, but until the tone in the relationship reaches boring levels, you are still happy with it despite the ups and downs. Melisa witnessed a roller coaster, which is more haphazard than the usual up and down of daily life. That she is hysterical does not help, because she loves to be the center of attention but is easily overwhelmed by situations, which makes her volatile and hysterical.

Turmoil in the relationship sets in when your dominant thoughts and feelings are negative rather than positive. For example, you may not be that interested anymore. Worse still, you may feel bored or regret when you think about the relationship.

You may start saying to yourself "I feel better without this relationship." The turning point to this mindset begins when a person starts looking for what is missing in his partner.

A catalogue of grievances may suddenly appear. And since what one looks for one sees, you will undoubtedly see the reasons to justify these grievances.

You draw onto yourself what you think and feel. It's the belief that is the object, not what you believe in. This mind principle of affirmation makes love and hate close neighbors; there is a very fine line between them and it's drawn because of how the mind works. Consequently, you can love or hate anything.

Physically, we own things because our minds affirm their existence through repeated thought and feelings. That is how you experience anything—by giving it attention!

So now that you are predominantly in a negative state of mind about this relationship, you begin to pull apart from each other. Notice how your mind does this again. You draw onto yourself what you feel and think about. So your mind through the affirmation principle will draw more negative thoughts, feelings, and conditions about your relationship. You pull more and more apart; at some point you start to feel separated, lonely, and unloved. Loneliness is emotional separation. It often comes from social withdrawal.

The amygdala is the area of the brain that deals with emotions, and it is not completely understood, so sometimes it's not easy to explain these things. In as much as emotions can be generally irrational, so sometimes there may not be a clear explanation for one's emotions. However, your subconscious mind has multiple filters about your disposition regarding the kind of person you may love, and these may trigger reactions through your natural instincts—gut feelings that even you may not be able to explain.

But remember that unconditional love is a dilemma It simply means that there are not external conditions or a secondary gain anticipated as a result of the two of you being together. In the same breath then, you can choose to love or not to love. You can say yes or no without feeling as if you owe him or her anything. You can do that without explanation. All you need to do is say, "No thanks." So, unless you reach the point where there is a specific commitment made to the other person, you do not have to feel obliged to move to a direction that is not consistent with your aspirations. And even after a commitment, you can still change your mind, nothing is forever. The difference here is that you do so with a lot of consideration and you do so to your best interest, without undue pressure.

Unconditional love is not a free pass, where when once you get in you are locked in for life. No. Some people play to that, doing whatever they feel like doing with the falsehood that your commitment is eternal. No. There is always the respect of boundaries. There is no limitless freedom. All you need to do is live up to the bargain, and hope that your partner handles the relationship in the same manner. If he or she does not, give the baboon the iron boot.

There are partners, as in Melisa's situation, who get abusive or do crazy things, such as exhibiting poor judgement or inappropriate behavior. On your own part, sometimes it's either a change in focus or expectations.

Waiting until you are ready for a commitment is very important. As you grow, your philosophy in life changes also changes as you become more mature. The kind of person you may want in a relationship or marriage when you are in your thirties, may be quite different from when you were in your twenties.

It could also be that the relationship was not meant for you. You can simply let go and move on.

Never feel pushed one way or another, because first you have to be happy with yourself—with or without a partner. The first rule of happiness is to feel good with yourself.

Some people go into a relationship or marriage not as equal partners, the way it's supposed to be, but with the feeling of having a vacuum or a defect that they think their partner will fill for them. When they end up not getting that false desire met, they get upset and frustrated and blame their partner.

This is one of the common reasons for people pulling apart rather than together in a relationship. And eventually the chain breaks.

If you know that you are whole, and feel good all the time, having a partner becomes a bonus, making you happier; but you are not solely dependent on it for your joyous life.

If you think about relationships in that way, you can breakup in one and walk away with your head high. If you actually love someone, you will wish that you were together, but if he or she makes the decision to move on, you may have no choice but to also move on. You only control part of this equation. It has to be mutual. You have to say to yourself it's better to be honest and move on than beat a dead horse for heaven knows how long. As for being emotional after a breakup, it's normal.

Short-term negative emotions in and of themselves are not bad; give it a few months and acknowledge the loss, do not deny it. Practice how to release negative experiences using the mirror exercise we have discussed. What causes long-term depression (more than two months) is trying to resist the loss. Loss is a normal part of life. The act of trying to resist is what brings nightmares and butterfly feelings in your stomach.

In order to gain freedom from toxic emotions, we have to learn how to guide them, because emotions can be quite irrational. To be in control is to be able to guide your thoughts and emotions. Since self-image is the anchor of emotions, creating a positive image within becomes the key. This is done by watching the kinds of beliefs that are entertained, because our self-image is formed from our internal dialogue. We have to constantly redirect our thoughts to reflect who we are. Look at the character flow chart in this book. It shows how our self-image flows from our identity and how our emotions are a projection of the picture that we have within.

I think that if Melisa would understand what loving or being loved means, and knew how to guide her emotions, she would not be so irrational in her approach to dating. I think that she would have a better dating experience and will be a better partner too.

Here is how it works. A positive self-image will make a person become the magnet or channel to dispense or manifest what comes from the soul-joy. That is how we allow our inner peace to flow. It first will shine from within, and then project to the external world.

In contrast, the thoughts that breed a negative self-image give rise to toxic emotions like resentment, bitterness, and anger. These are joy stealers. It is difficult to have inner satisfaction when our soul is encumbered by these toxic emotions.

It is not enough to believe in unconditional acceptance, we have to become a "soul practitioner" in order to release the peace that is within. Knowing about it without practicing it is merely intellectualization; we have to release it by living it.

Become a Soul Practitioner

To become a soul practitioner is to draw from our natural source of the soul, which like drawing water from a spring is an endless source. The soul is our joy. This comes with first believing in joy, and then practicing it. That is how it is released. We have to become the magnet or channel of whatever we seek in order to manifest it. Remember what you have learned on becoming a magnet of the quality you want to cultivate.

To believe without practice is simply intellectualization. We release the quality in question by putting it into practice. In that way, we do not just go through the motions. Rather, doing what we profess sets our body into motion. We get exhilarated and excited.

In order to create positive emotions of excitement, which tend to crowd out boredom from our lives, we should focus on the positive emotions of love and hope.

I do not know anyone who personifies love and hope more than Mother Teresa. She was humbled by the need that she saw on the streets of Calcutta. She found a niche. She made taking care of the very needy in society her life. In doing so, she made herself the channel for dispensing love and hope.

She became the soul practitioner. I think that if we focus on cultivating the three emotions of love, hope, and excitement, they will crowd out most of the toxic emotions that sap our joy. Love is the antidote of hopelessness, and excitement is the antidote of boredom.

If we constantly practice our internal dialogue that speaks to these three qualities, we will create a positive image that is consistent with them.

In essence, people go out and hurt someone, or say negative things, because they first think negative thoughts or hate, not love. Similarly, those who show compassion see giving in any form as virtuous. Their acts of generosity are first born from within, before they are manifested.

Most of the time people commit suicide it is because they do not see any hope for the future. People often feel unhappy because they think negative thoughts about something that they do not like or do not see a positive outcome to their life situation.

Excitement often comes with feeling self-control and moving toward the desired direction in our lives. In such circumstances, the person has interests that keep one energized and excited. Lack of interests leads to boredom and lack of inner satisfaction.

I am convinced that Mother Teresa's servant and caring attitude came from humility. She thought of others and their needs. She was not egotistic. It is not possible to give unconditionally when we are self-centered.

The saint of Calcutta is the consummate example of humility. She was not conceited or arrogant. She was very confident, because she believed in herself. Her faith in God also gave her more grounding and stability. Believing in something bigger than oneself has the tendency to take away the focus from our self, avoiding the sure fire recipe for making one prideful, which is the opposite of humility.

I think that a lack of humility and being egotistic are common obstacles to practicing the three greatest positive feelings—joy, love, and hope. Why is this important? Well, when we cultivate the quality of humility, it takes the focus off ourselves and inspires love (unconditional acceptance) and not greed.

Humility goes hand in hand with self-confidence, because you must accept yourself unconditionally. If you accept who you are without question, you are likely to offer the same to others, because you realize all humans, including yourself, have flaws. Once people reach that place where they realize that flaws are inevitable, they stop being pretentious. They can work on their weaknesses without feeling bad about it. They can say honestly that they do not know something without feeling nervous.

Exercise humility by thinking not of yourself, but of other people, and doing good to them. Continually live in that mindset, and see how a new world opens where you see needs to fulfill. Then watch how much more personal fulfillment you get in life.

That is how you allow the peace to shine, within and without. Could you imagine how many lives Mother Teresa changed by bringing hope? Of course, she became a beacon of hope. She inspired and dispensed hope.

Unconditional acceptance is a quality that we all have; we just have to release it. It is our basic nature, our soul. It is by expressing this that we release the life energy of joy, both for ourselves and for others.

We have to be disciplined in order to constantly act with unconditional acceptance. It is the icebreaker for everybody. It melts the hardness in our hearts. That is how we become a channel through which our joy and soul can be expressed.

Why should you accept and forgive people with their flaws? For the simple reason that love is the great overcomer, even of evil. To try to overcome flaws by fighting them is like fighting darkness with darkness. You cannot win like that. All you need is to bring the light of awareness, which makes the darkness disappear.

When you come across a porcupine, try touching the quills and see what they do to you. I know because my dog tried. I spent the whole day trying to pull them out, and she got more and more tortured. But I would not leave the quills in her skin.

Reacting to a situation is a slippery slope; you can easily be sucked into someone else's web of negativity because it is contagious. Acting with measured responses is more powerful. This is done by directing and redirecting our attention to what we wish to experience. Emotions can be very irrational if not tempered with choosing the thoughts that we desire.

Actually, that is where our power lies in programming our mind for joy. Develop a strong, quiet, inner spirit by focusing on the three most powerful emotions of love, hope, and excitement, and watch the magic in your life happens

The rationale for not resisting a negative situation is found in how the mind principle works. What we resist, we attract, because it only affirms or upholds what we profess. That is how we become hooked on negative emotions when we try to resist them. It cannot say no. it can only say yes. This is why unconditional acceptance is very powerful; not only is it the icebreaker that softens our hearts, it is in harmony with the mind principle.

7. A Future Steeled in Hope

Chapter 7:

A Future Steeled in Hope

"Fear defeats more people than any other one thing in the world."
- *Ralph Waldo Emerson*

The larger life mission, beyond survival itself, is important for giving the victim of adversity belief in the future. This larger life mission serves as a lifeline to the world beyond the present misery. Too often despair can leave us immersed in a quicksand of sadness. Repeatedly, hope proves to be more powerful than fear—real or imagined.

Hope is the feeling that events will turn out for the best. Also is the wish for something with the expectation that it will be fulfilled, believing that a better outcome is possible even when there is some evidence to the contrary.

Optimism is very close to hope in meaning it is a tendency to dwell on the most hopeful aspects of a situation. It is an outlook on life where one maintains a view of the world as a positive place, seeing the glass half-full of water as opposed to half-empty. Personal optimism correlates strongly with high self-esteem, with psychological well-being, and with physical and mental health. Optimism allows you to see the positive aspects of any situation and enables you to capitalize on each possibility. When you are optimistic and you see a negative event, you chose to dwell on the aspects of the situation that may lead to moving ahead, which is what's important. That is, you try to look for the silver lining in the situation. There's no question that hope and optimism are great sources of fuel for inner peace.

There is hardly a better example of a future steeled in hope than that of Victor Frankl. He is the author of the book *Man's Search for Meaning*. He talks about personal suffering and the eyewitness accounts of the excruciating pain inflicted on fellow inmates while he was imprisoned at Auschwitz for five years. In 1942, Frankl, a recently married psychiatrist, was arrested, separated from the rest of his family, and sent to the concentration camp. He observed that those who could emotionally survive their surroundings were those who could imagine themselves free to transcend the suffering and find a meaningful life despite the circumstances. It was on this premise that while in the prison camp, he secretly worked on a manuscript and imagined reuniting with his family. Instead of focusing on his lost purpose, Frankl created one. To survive horrors, people have to look into the future. His future would have been doomed if he had lost faith.

Hope is crucial because we never have direct answers for all problems;, learning how to handle negative situations is very important. Difficult life events can bring out the best in people if they choose to look for the silver lining in the situation.

Crises push people out of their comfort zone, which puts enormous pressure on them to perform. The urgency to perform makes them think out of the box. In that way, they brainstorm possibilities that they otherwise would not think of had they not been forced to. In such circumstances, your physiology, like the adrenaline thumping in your chest, enhances your performance. You can jump over a fence if you suddenly are being chased by a bear—something you may not have believed that you could do. The point is that accidently you prove yourself, and you know that you can do it, which increases your level of confidence and boldness. Why? Because you believe a little more about what you can really do.

Look at Frankl's situation; he did not have the power to reverse the situation in a physical way so he used his attitude to conquer adversity. He deliberately chose not to dwell on the apparent failure—becoming arrested and locked in a concentration camp. He created a new story filled with a new purpose, meaning, and significance to fill the "existential vacuum."

A spirit of optimism is uplifting all the time but especially in times of difficulty. The secret to this powerful psycho-spiritual fuel is to recognize the failure or potential failure, but to choose to dwell on something positive. No matter how dire a situation is, there can always be something positive on which to fixate your mind. Everything, including our thoughts or words we think and our actions, is energy. So rather that slipping backward with negative thoughts, why not choose to shift attention onto the worthy? This will make you expand and move forward into the future, which is empowering. Dwelling on the negative event, like wallowing in self-pity disempowers you because you slip backward and lose rather than gain strength. You only gain momentum and strength by moving forward.

I assert there are many problems that do not have solutions. Trying to solve all problems is like wanting to unring a bell once it's been rung. Shifting your mindset is the primary leverage for approaching any problem, whether there is a solution or not. If you do not use your imagination and you stifle your creativity when you cannot see beyond what is, then you are bound to follow a course of action that is merely guesswork.

The Peaceman, who migrated to North America from Bosnia fifteen years ago, is a typical North American because he has adopted the culture, language, and way of life. He struggled with life until he came to see me. That is when he saw the light. He left the darkness that had gripped him for many years. He got his future steeled in hope and spontaneously he resolved to evolve.

The main thing that held him back for those many years was the graphic image of watching his father beaten and killed during war. The horror would never leave his imagery. Whenever he lay in bed, he would continuously play the negative image in his mind. It got even worse when he tried to push back the negative image. He got flashbacks—scenes from the past. He simply could not focus because of these flashbacks. It took countless number of counseling sessions to reverse the situation.

I know that a major part of the solution lies on how Peaceman viewed the stressful event of watching his father killed. The emotional connection tends to be very strong when the negative event is graphic. This event occurs in the subconscious mind where long-term memory is stored. This area of the brain can spontaneously fire impulses independent of your conscious mind. This is why from Peaceman relives a negative experience that happened fifteen years ago flashbacks without conscious awareness. He found himself crying without any apparent cause for the same reason.

Peaceman's attempt to push back on the negative experience did not work. The right thing to do is acknowledge and release it. He had to do that in order to move his attention onto something positive. He had to create a new positive story, just as Frankl did. He had to find a new purpose to anchor his passion.

Finding inner peace was pivotal, because it would eventually put him into the path for any success that he wanted. As Esther and Jerry Hicks put it, the key to any kind of success is to first be happy. Until you do that, you are stuck and you cannot follow your bliss. That is how you release the energy of joy, which gives you the vitality that carries you through life.

Peaceman had so much emotional baggage that I figured out that to move forward he had to change his identity. He needed a major change in mindset. Even though he lived in North America, he was not yet adapted to the North American way of life. He eventually had to change his identity, mindset, name, culture, and his faith. He identified with the problems that he had in his life with his native country of Bosnia. In order to change the dynamics, he had to reinvent himself. He moved from the house he was living in. All the memorabilia that he had with him from Bosnia was discarded.

This was a very aggressive approach, but it was necessary if he wanted to find inner peace, because the essence of the process is to focus on who you are. Until his baggage was shed, like a pupa leaving its mantle behind it and emerging into its new world, he could not find peace, and no technique in the world would make any difference.

The soul is our natural and boundless source of vitality. It is well-being. It is expansive and abundant; you can call it anything virtuous or light, you name it. It is a limitless source of vitality, because there is no end to it. In order to access this endless source of vitality within you, you have to be in harmony with it. That is why awareness of the pathological nature and limitations of your ego is crucial. This is because your ego is limited, your soul is the true expression of who you are.

Emotional baggage and all beliefs that are incomparable with the soul constitute ego manifestations. They constitute the psychological resistance that eclipses the soul. The egoic self is most notable for its lack mentality. Anything that says to you that there is not enough or that something is inadequate or imperfect is the ego talking to you. It is very self-limiting because it sees impossibility, not possibility.

Faith is a great hope builder. Peaceman's change of faith from Muslim to Christian had a profound effect on him. He read scriptures every day. He took important verses and made them into affirmations that he repeated to himself every day.

Believing in something bigger than ourselves is very powerful as it rids us of our own burden, because too often our perception is clouded by our circumstances. That is why a strong belief in something greater than ourselves tends to build inner strength. Once the focus is taken away from our self, then we become more humble and caring of other people; these are qualities that add to our inner strength as becoming more humble is a measure of spiritual growth. The involvement here is not necessarily religion. No, it could be anything involving a cause that is bigger than you.

The image of the sun or light is likened to the spirit or virtue. Peaceman adopted this powerful image where the generosity of heart, wisdom, humility, love, and hope all come from. This light helped him dissolve the darkness that ruled his life before. He used to say he had no faith in any person or religion. After his awareness of the pathological nature of the egoic self, he realized that he was wrong. He remembers feeling like a coiled spring all the time because the resentment he harbored had transformed into cynicism, strife, envy, jealousy, impatience, hate, and much more. There is no way he could have been happy with these power stealers. They constitute emotional baggage. They zapped his energy and made him feel weak and powerless. He could only live a more vibrant life by leaving all this behind. This is because he learned how to put positive energy into the universe by expecting the best, thinking positive thoughts, and feeling good about himself and others.

One of Peaceman's problems was that he operated from the perspective of false humility. He believed in the myth that you need to worry about things in order to prove that you care. He tortured himself for many years before he would come to learn that if he cared about something enough, all he needed was to do something about it. Playing an active role in any situation makes you feel that you can positively affect the world. This refuels your can-do spirit. When you feel that you are a victim, it breeds helplessness, which is a recipe for worry and insecurity. If you learn not to be burdened by your circumstances and think more in terms of the wider purpose, you'll gain insight into how small your problems are. To reinvent oneself after a setback, putting things into perspective is important. Once you start seeing the bigger picture, other options emerge, and consequently, a plan for action. At that point, you'll stop resisting the setback, which leads to a lot of pain and wastes vitality because it focuses your energy on the past and not in the now or future. But the crowning step is to shift your attention to a new dream, as once your mind is preoccupied with a new dream it basically crowds out the baggage.

8. Fill Yourself with Passion

Chapter 8:

Fill Yourself with Passion

"I am supported and encouraged to follow my passion."

- Anonymous

Madi is a middle-aged man who came to see me because he was having difficulty dealing with negative people in his life. He was very unhappy about it. He was married with five children. He had a good job, friends, and had always been very enthusiastic about living, until boredom set in.

Madi started slipping backward into despair when he refused to do drugs with some of his friends. He ended up being alienated by his friends, and he took it too hard on himself.

Madi's life was pulling ahead in full swing until he faced a storm. He did not like facing it. Some people will have to face a setback in their lives. It could be a negative situation like in Madi's case. Or it could be as simple as frustration with a child's negative attitude.

My experience has been that many people like Madi are often doing very well in life until something happens that they do not like, then they begin to slip backward, lose their confidence, and enter despair, and unhappiness ensues. The key to living a life of excitement is to keep one's peace both in the good and bad times, so that you do not lose confidence.

The power is in using one's thoughts to reprogram the mind to stay on the bright side of life. Madi would have done better if he made a firm decision not to be pulled into the web of negativity of his friends. Instead he chose to be reactive to the situation, and what we resist we attract. So he attracted the negativity to himself. He lost his enthusiasm.

Madi stopped slipping backward into despair when he created a positive ethic for everything he did. He strived to do everything with great excitement and enthusiasm. He mastered how to become a magnet of what he wanted, as has been explained in this book.

He used the mirror exercises with affirmations that spoke to the essence of what he wanted to experience in his life. He understood that he would not overcome the evil of negativity with negativity as he did before. No. it was like trying to beat darkness away rather than bring on the light to make it disappear.

He created affirmations based on unconditional acceptance of the negative people he was facing in his life. Such acceptance is in harmony with the mind principle, it involves upholding and not resisting so he was not pulled into the web of negativity. Madi's power was in directing his thoughts by the choices that he made. He could not change his circumstances otherwise, not by changing his friends.

Staying on the bright side, and doing only what could make a difference, is a way of fanning one's flames of passion to keep going. Why? Because the ultimate goal is to make a positive impact for oneself and others. Thus, if an action is one that does not culminate to such an end, why execute it? It is wasted effort.

To stand against the forces of darkness, move your attention to the bright side—this light of conscious awareness is the key to influencing one's life in such manner as to live with enthusiasm. That is how people fill their minds with enthusiasm.

Madi adopted the candle as a positive image to follow. He made the affirmations, "Always on the bright side" and "Follow the light." He set the candle in front of him all day long as he worked. He set his mind on a positive ethic for work, taking care of his children, and much more. He was going to adopt excellence as his way of life. Everything he did, even doing dishes at home, he was determined to do excellently, and rather than worry about the negative people that he complained about, he accepted them unconditionally. The gracious attitude and appreciation rubbed off. Why? According to the mind principle, we uphold what we profess. So thinking loving thoughts makes us lovable. It all comes back to us. It was the resentment from Madi that was causing him heartache. The mind principle is very interesting because it throws whatever we think and feel back to us. The mind translates what we put into it back to us. So we have to be mindful of what we put in. That is how resentful people have sleepless nights. Their adrenaline levels go up because their stress level is raised. So, negative thoughts can change people's chemistry as well, for the worse.

People who master how to create enthusiasm live a richer and fuller life because even mundane activities can bring them a lot of excitement. They simply learn how to fill their heart with passion. They set themselves on fire. They fan their flames. How?

To be enthusiastic, use conscious awareness. Say to yourself that being passionate about everything you do is your way of life. All things begin with a thought. It has to be a way of life. In that way, it permeates your thoughts, behavior, and actions. This is important because the picture of an enthusiastic person has to first be seen within. Visualize yourself looking passionate, even about the most basic activities in life, so that you are not only passionate when you are doing what you consider fun. Everything for Madi was fun. He willed it in order to create it.

To be passionate, think enthusiastic. See yourself enthusiastic. That is how you create the picture within. See yourself as a source of light, not darkness. Imagine the radiation of joy coming out of you. That is how you set yourself on fire. Do not hold back, do whatever needs to be done with keen interest—the antidote of boredom. That action will set the body in motion. The adrenaline and endorphins are secreted to keep pace with the body's activities. These chemicals in turn boost energy and happiness respectively.

Living with passion is a mindset that could be cultivated. The seeds could be sown and nurtured. It is progressive as well as dynamic. It is also contagious, as it could be seen with Madi's case. Nobody enjoys being near negative people. Their negative energy and cynicism in interpreting everything negatively or having cryptic meanings draws people down.

It is important to be a generator of enthusiasm. Start by simply doing whatever you do flamboyantly. Sooner or later, you become passionate. But just having a look of eagerness is enough. It is not necessary to jump around. A quiet and strong personality is just as good. Go with what feels good for you, so long as you are in harmony with your basic nature. Visit the Character Flow Chart described earlier in this book once more.

A sense of humor like laughter and smiling can help dissipate a lot of stress, breaking the tension in the air; but humor is relative and sometimes others may not be drawn into the context easily and they may not see the point. But it is much better to be a source of enthusiasm by lifting people up, rather than pulling them down with negative talk or behavior. Acting with enthusiasm also inspires more of it. That is living it so that it is seen not heard. It is the positive words that we use, smiles and not frowns on our faces, the spring in our steps.

Passion is great enthusiasm. It is a feeling. It is the great fuel of life. Quite often people feel bored or uninterested because they lack passion for life. It is a very important quality to cultivate. It is possible to be a model of passion, simply by choosing to live a joyous life.

How people handle challenges speaks a lot to who they are. Challenges and setbacks in life are inevitable, so knowing how to deal with them is crucial. Learning how to deal with difficult situations puts a person far ahead in the game of maintaining peace of mind. The reason is that more often than not, people are happy if they have chosen to be, unless something bad happens and they lose their confidence as they slip into despair. If the downward spiral is not stopped, they eventually become unhappy.

Cultivating a mentally tough attitude is important. It builds inner strength that prepares you for the tough times. Review the area already discussed regarding the character traits that are important for maintaining inner peace: confidence, resilience, and perseverance.

Confidence, or the belief in one's abilities, makes us feel strong. Resilience is the ability to bounce back when we face a setback, and perseverance makes a person keep going despite all odds. These three qualities are crucial for a person to keep going forward in spite of the opposition, obstacles, and discouragement after a failure.

When a person does not have the ability to get up and dust himself off and keep going, he might sit back and wallow in self-pity. That is a sure recipe for creating a spiritual prison cell. In order to break away from such a mindset, one has to be able to challenge one's own belief when need be, because that leads to genuine growth and progress. It is a way of liberating one's energy because the alternative is to play the victim mentality, and what other people would do is contribute to building a prison cell for him, unless they are ready to challenge him to grow.

It is important to accept conditions that do not conform to one's ideals sometimes. It is important to set standards and stick to them, recognizing that sometimes we may not get what we want.

Learning to accept what life sets in front of us is very powerful. For example, just recognizing how fragile life is, and that it is temporary and unpredictable, because the end could come at anytime, makes us keep a rather loose handle on things, both spiritually and materially. That gives us feelings of calm and resignation, rather than those of anxiety and concern. The former attitude makes us relax and not take ourselves or little things too seriously. Being in an antagonistic and fighting mode all the time tends to sap our energy, and of course, our passion for life. We can only see the silver lining in a situation when we look for it, and even if all is lost, we can create a new objective that gives us a reason to live passionately.

Accepting the fact that problems are part of life, makes a person look at them differently. It could even be a way of proving oneself. How one looks at a situation is an important leverage in solving the problem. What one person may perceive as a glitch, may be seen by another person as a calamity.

Madi learned that his power was directing his attention to where he wanted by the use of thoughts and the choices that are made. By accepting the situation as it is, even a negative one, he gave his attention to the job at hand. In that way, energy was not spent trying to fight the situation.

Trying to change a negative situation is like wanting to unring a bell. It simply cannot be done. The key is to shift attention from the negative situation to something else. This could be accomplished very easily by creating a new story. Once the song is changed, the dance changes as well. It may be easier to create a new positive story if there is a silver lining, but not necessarily. You can create one or move to something totally new.

The key is to not deny the negative story, unless you have to. But acknowledging it is the easy way to release it. Do not dwell on the negative event either. Because when the story is told repeatedly, it eventually could become one's image. When somebody says, "I heard that you 'lost your hair' on the business deal," say "Oh, yes, I did, thank you for mentioning it," and then go back to bigger and better things. Do not start building a spiritual prison cell for yourself. When a person does that, he is choosing to act on his own terms and he can grow and gain a lot of strength, even from a negative situation. Constant practice can make a person see only glitches and not calamities, or see opportunity and not crisis.

Learning to stay on the bright side and not resist a negative situation is very important because quite often it leads to psychological suffering. Why? Because resisting a situation is how one becomes hooked into it emotionally and tortures oneself with the poison of negativity. The mind works by affirmation, so it only upholds what we profess. What we resist we attract. We will be emotionally hooked into a negative situation by resisting it. It is easy to avoid being sucked into a web of toxic emotions by dwelling on the bright side.

Passion for Others

I am not surprised when I find people who are not sure what to do with their lives. The reason is that I went through many years of drifting around too, without knowing exactly what I wanted to do. When I graduated from medical school in West Africa, I was twenty-eight years old. I came to Canada in 1994, and soon after became a Canadian citizen. I was very lucky to get into family medicine in Canada. After my training, I wanted to go into gynecology, as I had always wanted to. So even as I practiced family medicine, I did not really do it with a passion. I was divided between working and going back to school to specialize in gynecology.

My attention was divided because I spent a lot of time searching for a training position in universities in Canada and the USA. Luckily, a training position was given to be in Canada. I closed my medical practice, went back to school for six months. I found out after six months that it was not meant for me.

I have forever been grateful that I was given the opportunity to try out the specialty of gynecology; otherwise, I would have always had the false thinking that it was for me—I discovered it was not.

What I did not like about gynecology was the "rat race," or competitive attitude, among the doctors in the field. It was also a very stressful job. People were on the edge all the times. The feeling was like sitting on the needle all the time. The air was often filled with anxiety. The mindset was that of negative expectations. It always seemed like something bad would happen. It was just a matter of time, so they thought.

In 2007, I decided to cast the deciding vote for my future. Because I started appreciating family medicine for its variety and great quality lifestyle, I decided to go back to family medicine. I started seeing family medicine as a path to some of the things that I wanted to do in my life—my real passion, which was and is still philanthropy, notably in the area of poverty relief.

I realized in 2007, when I was forty-two years old, that for many years I had been drifting around without a strong passion for what I wanted in life. I was gripped by complacency, the false feeling of satisfaction because I already had a career. A new era dawned for me, and I started thinking more about others than myself. That was the turning point of my life, I would humbly say now.

I became motivated and driven about helping people, so I started a charitable organization for helping the hungry. I started a micro financing company in West Africa for helping the poor as well.

I understand why having a wider purpose beyond self is very important for being passionate. As a soccer coach, I know what it means to have the goal post in a soccer match. I always imagine what would happen if the twenty-two players in the soccer match would just dribble and dribble without having a goal post to score a goal.

Just think of how boring the match would be. Just look at the excitement that everybody has when a goal is scored. Everybody, the players and the fans, are excited. Does thinking about living a life without a purpose help to sharpen one's focus? That is how I was living before 2007. I had vague ideas about making a difference, but there was no specific commitment or action or specific plan.

Passion is a feeling. It is the fuel of life. It is a bigger force when we stand for something bigger than ourselves. It is a great way to harness our vitality. It is not enough to direct this great energy only to self. A person could be passionate about himself, but that is playing too small. It is like using a generator to light only one light bulb. Why not light a city? It just makes far more sense because it multiplies your efforts and the joy. Yes.

Direct the energy or passion toward something greater than self. At least having a goal will help harness the vitality without wasting it. Living out one's passion is how potential is released. That is how passion becomes real, by living is when a person conceives an idea in his or her mind. It's a dream, which when it moves from the head into the heart, becomes a passion. Living a passion feels even better, because of the sense of reward for one's self-service.

Drifting through life without passion is cheating oneself. Our life follows our thoughts, so if a person chooses to live a passionate life, it will happen. Passion is the great fuel of life, because it is the channel for releasing the life energy of joy and that leads to more personal fulfillment.

9. Develop a Forgiving Spirit

Chapter 9:

Develop a Forgiving Spirit

"The more resentment I release, the more love I have to express."

- Anonymous

I remember the story of a man who was sexually abused by his priest. This happened during his teen years. He is now in his forties, but has never forgiven the abuser. He never brought closure to the matter. Once in a while he went to court with the priest in an attempt to see whether he could be brought to justice.

He confided in me that each time he went to court, he felt a little bit better shortly after because he could sleep better, then the sleepless nights would come back after a few weeks. He went to bed with the priest on his mind every night. He was very bitter and resentful against the priest.

It was clear that this man was in misery, I often saw the tears rolling down his cheeks when he started saying anything about the priest. He worried about losing his dignity and much more. He had never brought closure to a negative event that happened about a generation ago. He still wallowed in self-pity.

Nobody in his or her right mind would condone the priest's actions, but to live in pure hell for a generation was even more pitiful. The vicious cycle of resentment that fed this young man with anxiety, stress, and baggage that he clung to made his life miserable.

This young man lost his freedom because he lacked self-control; he was acting according to the priest's will and not his. He just simply could not enjoy his life in that state of mind. The joy stealers like anger and resentment he carried against the priest were sapping his passion for life. That is why he was flat, bored, and saw no reason to live.

At some point in our lives, each of us faces a betrayal of one sort or another. The psychological and emotional reaction that follows such disloyalty at first may see insurmountable, until we decide to forgive. Having a forgiving spirit is letting go of the past, especially events that are deemed negative.

Forgiveness is a very empowering and healing process because it dissolves the negative emotions of hate, guilt, and regret that come with an unforgiving spirit. It is the negative emotions (toxic emotions), that draw psychological pain or suffering into a person's life. These emotions are toxic, because in reality they are poisonous to our body.

True forgiveness is unconditional acceptance. It is a letting go process of the negative event, like the sexual abuse here, without assigning blame to anybody. It is very self-empowering because a person who forgives, experiences psychological release. Hence, they do not feel chained to the event anymore. Psychological closure then happens.

An unforgiving spirit is very painful because what we resist, we attract, according to the mind principle of affirmation. So a person gets hooked onto the negative event, whether it is real or imagined. The psychological resistance created in the form of toxic emotions of resentment, hate, anger, guilt, and regret sap his energy.

That is how a person draws psychological suffering onto himself, by reacting against a negative event.

A lot of a person's life energy of joy is trapped in the toxic emotions described above. Resenting and hating is vitality wasted. People lose sleep in the process because their stress level goes up and more adrenaline is secreted by the body. Small physiological amounts of adrenaline would enhance a person's performance. But in very stressful situations, a lot more than the physiologically tenable levels are discharged. This is what leads to insomnia and anxiety. That is the butterfly feeling or knot in the stomach or sweaty palms that people feel when anxious. A fast heartbeat or high blood pressure may also occur.

So we can see how lack of forgiveness negatively affects our health and inner peace. Why? Well, because we certainly are not at peace with the signs of stress and anxiety described above. There is no absence of anxiety within. So we are not manifesting our innate well-being or joy. This is why when a person forgives, he or she gains his or her energy back. It is a great process for releasing our otherwise-trapped energy, in the form of toxic emotions.

Toxic emotions are very poisonous because they hold people back. They are joy stealers. A person cannot fully experience joy energy when he or she is trapped in the past, because he or she is not living in the moment. In order to be able to direct and redirect our thoughts, we have to be fully present. This is very important because emotions can be irrational, so they need to be guided with thought.

This young man was vindicated through the main benefit of having a forgiving spirit. He reclaimed his life energy of joy that had been outsourced by being emotionally chained to the priest.

He learned how to use the techniques described in this book on how to direct his attention. He also learned how to use the mirror exercises and affirmations to develop a more forgiving spirit.

First, he learned to not resist any negative situation, by simply acknowledging it and letting go, without dwelling on it for too long. He also stopped talking about sexual abuse to his friends. He could only discuss important aspects of it with his therapist.

The second thing he did was change the dance, and in order to do so he first had to change the song. So he created a new positive story, his life story.

The third thing was then to create affirmations based on his new story. He then repeated them to himself all day long. That was his new conditioning. The repetition supplanted the affirmations into his subconscious mind—the seat of long-term memory. This is very powerful because the mind works through affirmations. He visualized himself in front of the mirror in order to reinforce the new positive and joyous image, one that was devoid of the priest. That is how he took off the emotional chain to his past. He broke away from the "baggage" that was sapping his energy, making him live in hell—his own self-created spiritual prison cell. He had to disidentify with the past. The problem with being hooked on the negative event is that it takes over one's life. It became his identity, who he was. Look at the character chart and see how self-image flows from identity and how our emotions are anchored on our self-image.

It is very important to put a negative event in the right perspective. Otherwise it could take over one's life, like this young man. He lived in hell for a generation until his therapist broke the vicious cycle where he created toxic emotions that kept him away from a joyous life. It is simply wrong to identify with a setback like that. He needed to identify with who he really was; what resonated with his core values and belief system.

Sometimes there can be a triumph from even seemingly tragic circumstances if a person looks for the silver lining. Even when there is none, a person can cease to dwell on the negative event at least. That would shift attention to the worthy. Redirecting one's attention in such manner is our ultimate power and control, which inspires inner satisfaction. Why? Because we feel good about ourselves when we feel in control and our joy energy is not trapped in the form of toxic emotions.

To direct one's attention to whatever he or she chooses to experience is to act on one's terms, and that is freedom. In that way, a person can gain a lot of strength and growth even from a negative event. So, rather than deny a negative event that happened in one's life, acknowledge it in order to release it. Do not dwell on it. Stick to the new positive story. That is the way to change the dance, by first changing the song.

To accept events and people unconditionally is an effective way to sidestep toxic emotions that tend to sap our spiritual, psychological, and emotional energy. That is self-empowering because ultimately our power lies in choosing the right thoughts. So reaching for the good-feeling thoughts is programming our mind for joy.

10. Cultivate a Joyous Feeling

Chapter 10:

Cultivate a Joyous Feeling

"I am willing to allow joy to enter my life."

- Anonymous

Throughout this book, I have described how a person can use both thoughts and actions to improve on his or her joyous state of mind. The reason is that becoming joyous will help a person achieve greater personal fulfillment by living a richer and fuller life.

There may be people who can achieve this state of mind naturally, but I know that constant practice will make it even better, especially when a person can measure the level of growth and discipline. In order to grow, it is important to challenge oneself to take positive steps and to be disciplined. It is not enough to be willing to allow joy to enter into one's life, although it is an important step because it has to be willed by use of one's volition. People have to be willing to become a channel or magnet of whatever they profess in order to make it happen. Those who read this book will benefit more if they start by assessing their level of discipline on how often they use the principles described in this book. It should be a daily practice. It can be used for devotion at any time of the day that is convenient—to supplant the concepts into the subconscious mind through repetition so they become a habit. That how these principles will become second nature and intuitively become part of our way of life with minimal conscious effort.

The first step in achieving anything starts with our thoughts. A person first has to understand inner satisfaction, that state of mind without feeling tension within. This is important because people think about the things that they believe in, but in order to achieve results both attention and action must be directed to that end. That is how people evolve and expand, through learning how to cultivate emotions or excitement as I have outlined, that will strengthen, nurture, and preserve what they already have. There is a continuous growth process involved. That is why living a life of personal fulfillment is a journey, not a destination.

There is a need for disciplined practice in order to achieve growth in the area of inner satisfaction. A person can force him or herself to grow by simply keeping a log of how disciplined he or she is on a daily basis on following through on the different things that I have described for spiritual development. Be honest with how much change has happened over a specific period of time. For example, did the score change from a three to an eight on the scale of one to ten? And, has it translated to a corresponding tune-up in the level of satisfaction?

We learn from wise people that we make hay when the sun is shining. So the kinds of qualities that we cultivate for mental toughness need to be done now, because setbacks, calamities, negative events, and negative people do not announce their coming. The key is to be determined not to be pulled into the web of negativity that is a sure recipe for toxic emotions that sap vitality. To do that is to practice self-preservation. We all have a baseline of joyous feelings that we need to defend.

We become what we want by first becoming the channel or a magnet for it. Becoming joyous is a great fruit that needs cultivation. We have to possess it if it is to flow from our spirit to us and others. It cannot come from emptiness. The spirit is intangible, but its manifestations are tangible.

Being a nurturer of others and ourselves is important. Emotions that we carry resonate within us, and whether they are positive or negative, we first feel the effects. So when we nurture others, the effect often rubs off on us too. And there are psychological benefits too. The prideful feeling of giving of one's service is very sweet.

We can practice the joy of caring for other people, especially when what we give is done unconditionally. People enjoy caring for others. I do too. It feels good. Caring for others feels good to the extent that we want, but caring people need to establish boundaries, otherwise they are taken for granted. And caring people need to offer their service without pressure on others because everybody has volition and freedom to choose what he or she wants. We all have to be instruments of our own destinies. We can only help others help themselves. They determine their destiny, not us. We cannot force others to be joyous. They have to decide whether they like it and whether they will do what it takes to get it.

Why is unconditional acceptance so powerful and peaceful? It is a great way to sidestep the toxic emotions that come when we try to resist negative events or people. Also, unconditional acceptance takes away the focus from self. More often than not, people feel unhappy because they first think negative thoughts. A negative internal dialogue is what leads to a negative self-image. The thoughts of inadequacy and emptiness that result from self-pity are a recipe for building a spiritual prison cell for ourselves. At some point, we feel like we are in a hole. We feel emptiness within. That is how we outsource our joyous spirit, by dragging ourselves down into a hole!

People have to learn to recharge their batteries before they get too low. We take our cars to the garage because we want to avoid calamity on the highway. We do not wait until our gas tank is totally empty before we fill it up. So why don't people tune themselves up spiritually on a daily basis? This book could be used for that. We do not need to wait until we are overcome by anxiety, stress, or depression before we act. We can build inner strength all the time, when we have the opportunity—we can practice! I know how important this is, as a physician, because illness often comes on because the body is facing strain of one sort or the other. Whether it is physical, psychological, emotional, or otherwise, any invasion can permeate our body through the spirit, mind, or body. They are interconnected. That is why we can tell our body what to do by our thoughts or by our actions. We just need to tell it long and often enough and it will happen. How? The cells in our brain are connected to the cells in our body through the autonomous nervous system of nerves, neurotransmitters, chemicals, and hormones. This is very important, because we can then understand why stress affects the body from head to toe. It increases the secretion of chemicals, like adrenaline, which get both our heart rate and blood pressure up. More acid also is secreted in our stomachs, which leads to ulcers. The effects are multiple, but it's important to just understand that there is a connection.

But how does this work? Well, people speak to themselves more than they do to other people, throughout the day and even in their sleep. The subconscious mind works all through our lives, even when we are asleep. It is important for people to listen to the conversation within. Simply ask the question, "How am I feeling right now? Relaxed? Tense?" If what is causing distress first is not acknowledged, it will not be released. This is why it is important to direct attention within to the functioning of our body. If letting go of the thought that is causing the distress doesn't work, the next step is to change the internal dialogue from a negative to a positive one. Just doing that will tip our energy positively. And soon we are relaxed, then we smile or even laugh. If those strategies do not work, use others. Review the different techniques described in this book.

It is very important to see the connections because that will motivate their use. And cultivating a joyous life involves multiple things.

So, recognize the fact that choosing good-feeling thoughts that are uplifting can boost the secretion of happy chemicals like serotonin and endorphins. And laughter and exercise can do the same thing.

In the end, the feeling of joy is a state of mind. It will follow the great mental law, the mind principle, which works by upholding what we hold in our imagination—real or imagined.

This law governs thinking, the same way that the law of gravity rules the physical universe. What you think upon, inevitably grows. Thoughts are therefore causes, and the conditions in your life are effects. If you want to know the quality of your thoughts, you need only look at your conditions, like your feelings, the kind of car that you ride, or what you have or don't have.

The more you think of yourself as joyous, the more exuberant you will be.

About The Author

Dr. Alfred Nkut, M.D., is an accomplished physician, entrepreneur, and philanthropist with avid interest in leadership. His experience has shown him that self-improvement, especially development of character goals, is not emphasized in most formal educational systems. For this reason, he grew increasingly interested in studying, learning, growing, and researching to provide additional insight into the subject of leadership.

Dr. Nkut sees every day as an opportunity to add value not only to his own life, but to the lives of others as well. He has also founded the Skylimit Corporation to make a difference in the lives of people, and a financial institution in Cameroon, West Africa with the goal of poverty relief.

The more he learns and understands the area of leadership and success, the more passion he has for sharing that knowledge and for encouraging those who wish to improve their lives. He knows of no better way to get a kick out of life than to give, because for him giving is receiving; it is love—and that's how you make your way to "heaven."

Dr. Nkut and his wife, Dr. Elaine Blacklock, both practice medicine in Greater Sudbury, Ontario, Canada, and are proud to call the city home along with their children Jacob and Ruthie.

**Other Books
By Dr. Alfred Nkut:**

Leadership For Success:
Dynamic Model of Influence
(Release Spring 2010)

The Art of Happiness
(Release Summer 2010)

Dream & Succeed:
An Inspirational Day Book
(Release Fall 2010)

Eight Secrets to Healthy Living
(Release Winter 2010)

www.alfrednkut.com

LaVergne, TN USA
13 July 2010
189428LV00001B